Frances Power Cobbe

Alone to the alone

Prayers for atheists

Frances Power Cobbe

Alone to the alone
Prayers for atheists

ISBN/EAN: 9783743355132

Manufactured in Europe, USA, Canada, Australia, Japa

Cover: Foto ©Lupo / pixelio.de

Manufactured and distributed by brebook publishing software (www.brebook.com)

Frances Power Cobbe

Alone to the alone

Alone to the Alone;

PRAYERS FOR THEISTS,

BY

SEVERAL CONTRIBUTORS.

EDITED, WITH A PREFACE,

BY

FRANCES POWER COBBE.

"Let us invoke God himself, not in mere form of words, but by elevating our souls to Him by prayer. And the only way truly to pray is to approach alone the One who is Alone. To contemplate that One, we must withdraw into the inner soul, as into a temple, and be still."
Plotinus, 5th Ennead, Lib. i.

"This is the life of the blessed,...to seek, alone, Him who is Alone."
Ibid., 6th Ennead, Lib. ix.

Second Edition.

WILLIAMS AND NORGATE,
14, HENRIETTA STREET, COVENT GARDEN, LONDON;
AND 20, SOUTH FREDERICK STREET, EDINBURGH.

1872.

LONDON:
PRINTED BY C. GREEN AND SON,
STRAND, W.C.

PREFACE.

THIS book is designed for the use of those who desire to cultivate the feelings which culminate in Prayer, but who find the rich and beautiful collections of the Churches of Christendom no longer available, either because of the doctrines whose acceptance they imply, or of the nature of the requests to which they give utterance. Adequately to replace in a generation such books, through which the piety of ages has been poured, is wholly beyond hope. The ambition to achieve such an enterprize would but betray ignorance of the laws by which these precious drops are distilled slowly, year after year, and century after century, from the great incense-tree of humanity. But if as yet, and for a long time to come, the literature of Theism must be comparatively poor and unmellowed, it does not follow that we ought not to commence, as best we may, the task of producing its earlier fruits; trusting reverently in the Power which, we believe, is guiding the souls of men to a holier and happier faith than the world has yet known, to give to us by degrees all the treasures of noble thought and sacred inspiration. If our religion be genuine, it must needs happen that, at its proper stage of growth, it put forth bud of prayer and flower of praise, not in artificial imitation of those which have grown on another stem, but fresh from its own heart, and "bearing seed after its kind." With the conviction that such blossoming is even now taking place in hundreds of souls from east to west of the globe, I have endeavoured to gather from the friends best known to me such prayers as they were willing to lend; especially such as they might have written at any time under the influence of those more vivid feelings which we all desire to perpetuate. The result of a compilation so formed is, of course, in every sense, imperfect and fragmentary. Little effort has been made to fill up obvious deficiencies; and none at all to modify either in favour of more conventional phraseology, or of the editor's personal opinions, the expressions which each writer has spontaneously chosen. In no degree are the Prayers offered as models of what such compositions *ought* to be, but only as what *are* the aspirations of living souls. Perhaps in the great solitude wherein most of us dwell for the larger part of our lives, as regards all our deeper emotions, it may be more helpful to know that other human hearts are feeling as we feel, and thinking as we think, rather than to read far nobler words, which come to us only as echoes of the Past. That a strong likeness of sentiment runs through the various pieces in this volume, has seemed to me, as I received them one after another, to shew in a remarkable way the essential identity of Theism, whether embraced by old or young, men or women, Europeans or Asiatics; by minds trained in the schools of Christianity or of Heathenism, of the Roman Church, or the Anglican, of the Calvinist or the Unitarian. The bonds of authority once broken, and the soul set at liberty to find its God, it would appear (if the search be one of the heart and life, as well as of the intellect) that the conclusions arrived at by the seekers do not very essentially differ, no matter from how remote a point of the theological compass they originally started.*

Perhaps it will be asked, "Why make formal manuals of Prayer? Do Theists need such aids to lift up their hearts; and cannot they dispense with helps which better become the puerile than the manly stages of the religious life?" I answer, that I can believe there

---

* Perhaps it may be as well once for all to state that fifteen persons have contributed to this book. With the exception of two Prayers taken from the excellent little Manual of M. Leblois of Strasbourg, they are all now published for the first time. It is earnestly requested that the reader will not endeavour to identify their respective authorships.

may be happy souls who have transcended any such need, and for whom other men's prayers would be superfluous and intrusive. But I have not yet known in actual life one who can always soar into the upper air of thought, and feel no flagging wing, no need to be sustained and strengthened at intervals by the aid of his brother. It is true that the man who never addresses his Father in heaven, save in words dictated to him by his priest, has not yet learned to pray at all. But, on the other hand, the man who feels no kindling of his heart as he joins in the worship of his fellows, seems to me to have either ascended far above, or fallen below, the average of human sentiment. Because we have found a religion which satisfies alike our hearts and intellects, we have not, therefore, altered the conditions of our moral constitution, or passed outside the realm of those beneficent laws of sympathy which knit together the sons of men in mutual help and mutual dependence. It is subjecting our faith to an unnatural strain, a strain which only the fulness of intellectual and spiritual assurance can enable us to bear, to forego all the ordinary aids of piety; and I, for one, cannot but regret that we, of all men who believe in God, most rarely meet together to worship Him; that our reserve in such matters keeps us so far apart, that we lack all brotherly help and sympathy in the struggles of life; and, finally, that we have no books in whose perusal we can wholly thrust aside that necessity for criticism which is our burden and our bane.

Again, is it asked, Why not use the grand, time-sanctified collects and litanies of Christendom, merely omitting from them any words we cannot conscientiously follow, and substituting here and there a new phrase for an old? I reply, that such maimed and mutilated prayers are very far from fulfilling my idea of a genuine religious utterance. The familiar and venerable words, rudely docked in one place and corrected and modernized in another, are to me painful both to ear and heart, like a dear old tune whose cadence is destroyed. Nor is this all. Though all true piety has the same essential character, and we can joyfully sympathize with it, breathing alike in the words of Hebrew prophet, Roman sage and Christian saint, yet each great faith must have a language which is peculiarly its own, and in that tongue alone can its full meaning be expressed. Were Theism merely the popular creed of Europe with its most unsightly excrescences cut away, were it simply the old creed trimmed by closer logic, then indeed it would well become us to make our worship also the curtailed and amended repetition of the old forms. But the real state of the case is the reverse of all this. Theism is not "Christianity *minus* Christ," nor Judaism *minus* the miraculous legation of Moses, nor any other creed whatsoever merely stripped of its supernatural element. It is before all things the positive affirmation of the Absolute Goodness of God; and if it be in antagonism to other creeds, it is principally because of, and in proportion to, their failure to assert that goodness in its infinite and all-embracing completeness. This being so, it is impossible that the liturgies of other religions can afford suitable expressions of Theistic faith and love, or that it can suffice to abbreviate or alter them to make them fit our needs. They are indeed beautiful and venerable beyond any words I need use to praise them. In numberless instances they breathe a simple directness of faith, a fervour of penitence and devotion, at which our cold hearts must stand rebuked. As it has been the Theism in Judaism, in Christianity, and in every other great religion of the world, which has been its inner life and principle of vitality, so with joy we recognize the true Theistic spirit of filial love and loyalty continually bursting out through all their formularies. Spontaneously our highest feelings for ever find expression in the words which have fallen from Jewish or Christian lips during three thousand years of prayer; and never can we conceive of a time arriving when some of the Hebrew Psalms, and some of the English Collects, will be surpassed and left aside. But because we rejoice in these relics of ancient piety, and delight to use them as often as they suggest themselves as the genuine expressions of our feelings, and love to link ourselves by their employment to the great chain of pious souls stretching through the Past, it does not therefore follow that we can confine ourselves within their limits, or find in them, as a whole, the free channel wherein our faith can flow unbrokenly.

And now, to turn to a deeper question than all these,—one that lies at the root of the whole matter: Is there any use in Prayer at all? Is not the attempt at direct intercourse between the poor, feeble soul of man on earth, and the awful, incomprehensible Power behind the veil of creation, a presumption and a delusion? Is not Prayer one of the many errors of the past which it behoves the disciples of an enlightened philosophy to relinquish? Controversy of any kind is very far from being the purport of this book; but on this point, which concerns its own rational meaning, I must needs speak as fully and as strongly as I am able. I shall do so the more earnestly because, as I understand it, the whole character of our religion turns on this hinge; and if I were asked to describe what I considered the only important difference between the numberless minds whose mental latitude now lies between Atheism and authoritative Christianity, I should say that it was defined by the deep line between Theists who pray and Theists who do not pray. To the former, Theism is a Religion,—as I deem it, the truest, purest, happiest of all the religions of earth. To the latter, it is a Philosophy,—a refined, liberal and ennobling Philosophy; but not a Religion, and tending, I fear, to recede ever further from all that constitutes a Religion.

Two errors seem constantly to beset mankind in treating of the nature of our knowledge of God. On one side there are men who look on the intellect as if it were an unholy hand, wherewith it is profane and impious to touch the Ark of Faith. On the other side are men who consider it as the proper and sole organ of religious knowledge, and say that unless they can firmly grasp and freely handle the shrine, they will pay it no honour.

Both these views are surely partial and misleading. The intellect and understanding are divine gifts, as much as the conscience and religious sentiment are divine gifts, and have their right equally to assert themselves. But it does not follow, because an organ of mind or body is sound and its revelations deserving of attention, that it is therefore the express and proper organ for the recognition of any special class of truths. The eye, for example, is the proper medium for one kind of knowledge; the ear for another. Nothing could be more absurd than to attempt to study acoustics primarily through the means of those experiments by which sound can be made to produce visible results; or, on the other hand, to put out our eyes because we cannot through them discern music. So far as I can perceive, these are precisely the two mistakes men make about religion. Men of science commonly study religious phenomena merely through the intellect; and trace God, not by His voice in their hearts, but through the visible results of His power in the external world. Devout Christians listen reverently to the voice, but close their intellectual eyes, thereby losing the salutary correction of the first sense by the second. The lesson we have now to learn seems to be to avoid both these errors. We have to take it to heart that it is the soul itself which must bear witness to the things of the soul, the conscience which must reveal our moral Law, the specific sentiment of Religion which must bring us to God. And when this is thoroughly understood, then the share which the intellect ought to take in our theology will equally be apparent. It will be (to return to our simile) precisely analogous to that which the sense of sight takes in the study of sounds. When our eyes see somewhat which apparently contradicts the report of our ears, we are led to pause and inquire which sense is conveying the more correct testimony. We may, for example, hear a sound which we mistake for thunder; but seeing the smoke of artillery, we soon learn that our first impression misled us, and that it was not the powers of heaven, but of earth, which had disturbed us. Or, on the other hand (and as much more often happens in the spiritual life), if our eyes behold no living being in the twilight which has gathered round us, and we are ready to cry, "I am utterly alone!" and yet at that moment hear a deep, low breath, like the pulsations of a living heart beside us, or a "still, small voice" speaking to us out of the silence and the gloom, then we rely no more on the testimony of our dim eyes, but say in awe-struck tones, "Lo, God is in this place, and I knew it not."

It is but natural that the Father of Spirits should speak to us directly through our spirits, rather than through the medium of the outer world. If there be any truth at all in what has been called "the hypothesis of a God," I do not see how thoughtful men can overlook the fact, that that hypothesis itself almost involves the conclusion that the highest part of man must be in nearer contact with Deity than the lower; that in the Will, the Conscience and the Affections, we must reach God more directly than through the inductions of the Intellect from the reports brought to us by our senses of the external world. The endless mistakes and errors into which mankind have fallen in this matter, do not disprove the immense presumption in favour of such relation between the Infinite and finite spirit. They only shew that human nature spontaneously believes in it so soon as it rises above the merely animal condition; and that it also needs the proper work of reason and conscience to save it from such aberrations.

Thus, then, I conceive the true Method of religious inquiry is the converse of that which men of science in our day commonly follow. Instead of beginning with the outward world of matter, and seeking God primarily in the phenomena of nature, in the laws of gravitation and electricity, and in the mysteries of the first existence of species, of organic life, of the stellar nebulæ, I hold that we need to find Him first in the human soul, and then, and hardly till then, to see the traces of His wisdom and power throughout the universe. I conceive that, as a matter of fact, it is more than doubtful whether man would have ever found God in nature if he had not first found Him in his own heart; and I think that all the arguments which are supposed to prove the existence of a Deity have not derived their force from coming to us as fresh logical syllogisms, but because they corroborate what we already inwardly dimly feel to be true. As it has been well said of the great collateral doctrine of a future life, we do not believe it because we have proved it, but we for ever seek to prove it because we believe it. We endeavour to see with the eye of the intellect that which we have heard with the inward ear of heart and conscience. Having known the great Painter or Sculptor by personal intercourse, we gaze at his works and rightly conceive that we see in them the character of mind which we are already aware belongs to him. But to construct a true idea of the Painter out of his picture, the Sculptor out of his statue (a single picture and a single statue, be it remembered, in the infinite gallery of the systems of suns), is more than any ingenuity of criticism could accomplish; and the attempt to do it almost inevitably leads to gross mistakes.

The evidences of Divine work presented by the physical universe seem indeed vast when taken at their proper value as secondary to the phenomena of the moral world. Thrusting aside, as beyond our ken, all speculations about the First Cause of existence, or the proper Eternity or absolute Omnipotence of God, there remains in the true field of human science the materials for an immeasurable cumulative proof of the presence, everywhere throughout the planetary systems, throughout the inorganic world, throughout all vegetable and animal life, of a Will analogous in some of its most definite characters to a human Will, and differing therefrom essentially only in its transcendent Wisdom, and in a certain stupendous Patience which bespeaks the consciousness of the boundless Time wherein it works. Our love of Order, of Variety, of Beauty, are all there, traceable in that great invisible Force; insomuch that even men who refuse to give to it the name of God can never write of it without some phrase about Nature "designing" or "accomplishing" somewhat, which only a Living Will can be conceived (without a metaphor) to design or accomplish. To the taunt that man thus "makes a

God in his own image," we reply, that he does it for the valid reason that he traces through all the works of God characteristics essentially human, though magnified to the scale of Deity.

To undervalue the testimony which the material world bears to its Maker, would be the last error into which a Theist should fall. That beautiful and glorious creation must be for ever dear to us as the "garb we see Him by." Nay, we conceive that we may joy in its revelations of wisdom, and its scenes of grandeur and beauty, more than other men may easily do, tracing in them something beyond the bare facts of such wisdom and beauty, even the truths to which they witness regarding a Being nearer and dearer than flower or star. But again, I repeat, all that this outer world can teach us, is but the corroboration of the lesson taught in our own hearts, and in the record of what our fellow-men have been taught in their hearts, since true Human Nature arose out of its brute and barbarian origin. All the monitions of conscience, all the guidance and rebukes and consolations of the Divine Spirit, all the holy words of the living, and all the sacred books of the dead,—these are our primary Evidences of Religion. In a word, the first article of our creed is, "I BELIEVE IN GOD THE HOLY GHOST." After this fundamental dogma, we accept with joy and comfort the faith in the Creator and Orderer of the physical universe, and believe IN GOD THE FATHER

Almighty, Maker of Heaven and Earth. And, lastly, we rejoice in the knowledge that (in no mystic Athanasian sense, but in simple fact), "*these two are One.*" The God of Love and Justice who speaks in conscience, and whom our inmost hearts adore, is the same God who rolls the suns and guides the issues of life and death.

If these views of the proper grounds of religious knowledge be near the truth, it follows that nothing can be more unphilosophical and unscientific than to study theology primarily as a series of intellectual problems to be solved by induction. Of course it is open to any man to assert that our intellectual faculties are alone reliable, and our spiritual faculties fallacious and deceptive, and that what cannot be proved intellectually cannot be really known at all. But the answer is obvious, that on such a principle much more must be excluded from human life beside Religion, even all that concerns the affections and the imagination. No one can prove Love or prove Beauty. No one can demonstrate that a picture or statue or poem or piece of music is beautiful, or the starry sky sublime. No one can drive us into affection for our friend by a syllogism. He who admits that there exist in us other and equally valid faculties beside those of the intellect, cannot logically affirm the exclusive or supreme right of the intellect to judge in matters spiritual, any more than in matters æsthetic or in those concerning the affections. From various points of view, it may be maintained that all our faculties are untrustworthy. Nothing is easier than for one school of thinkers to shew cause why we should disbelieve our bodily senses; while it is the common opinion of others, that they alone deserve reliance. But the rational presumption assuredly is, that all our faculties are valid as regards their proper objects; or, as Mr. Martineau has expressed it, that they are "true all round," though of course all liable to error. The opposite hypothesis, that a faculty inherent in human nature may be essentially false and wholly deceptive, is outrageous. To admit that the hand and the eye afford true evidence of palpable and visible objects, but to deny that the spiritual part of man bears equally true witness of spiritual realities, is an anomaly which could only be justified were there anything essentially absurd in the testimony so received. It is no justification at all for refusing it, that its truth is not absolutely demonstrated by any other faculty.

Thus it is explained why many inquirers in our day vainly go on sifting the phenomena of the physical world, as if the Divinity were something hidden like a lump of gold in the quartz. They are on a wrong line of search altogether, and the whole method of their inquiry is vicious and illogical. They look *without*, for what must first be found *within*.

What, then, is the true method of this divine

search? The question may be answered easily. How should a man study music, painting or poetry, or how become a mathematician or a geologist? How indeed, but by cultivating the special faculties concerned in such pursuits, and developing that side of his nature which turns to the Beautiful or the True? It is no mysticism, but plain common sense, to say that Religion must be treated in the same way, and that our inward ear must be attuned like the ear of the musician, and our spiritual eye trained to see as the eye of the painter. The care, the practice, the reverence, which are so needful in one case, cannot be dispensed with in the other.

But to what conclusion, then, have we arrived, and to what does all this reference to natural analogy amount, save to the fact, that if we desire to find God we must lead that moral and spiritual life which is a life of Prayer, the indirect prayer of sustained moral effort after a godly life, and the direct prayer of approach to God in heart?

Is there anything mysterious or difficult to believe in all this? Surely not so, once we have admitted the postulate that there exists a Being with whom our higher natures, our wills and consciences, bear a nearer affinity than our bodily frames. On the contrary, there is a strong antecedent presumption that our Creator should have so constituted us, as that such self-upraising on our part should be the condition of our consciousness of Him, and that He should require us to come into the sunshine of His presence when we desire to be warmed and enlightened. Such mechanical action of Deity in the realm of spirit as should dispense with all such conditions of effort on our part, and bestow the holiest gifts indifferently on every struggling saint and every careless sinner, would be utterly foreign to all we know or can imagine of the principles of Divine government. We cannot suppose that God should act upon a living soul as upon a senseless and irresponsible clod, and press down both alike with an equiponderant and unvarying gravitation. For the unconscious matter there is the rigid law. For the conscious spirit there must be—not an absence of all law, but—the agency of a law which shall take its moral freedom into account.

Prayer is, in its highest form, literally the "communion" of the Divine and human spirit; and for communion to exist, it must needs be that two concomitant wills be exerted, the will of him who speaks, and that of him who listens, of him who asks, and him who grants; and again, in converse shape, of him who inspires, and him who reflects inspiration, him who bestows grace, and him who receives it. To forget this truth, and speak, on the one hand, as if religious "exercises" (as they are called) were all our own self-acting, self-reflecting spiritual gymnastics, or, on the other hand, to expect that God will bestow His best gifts on our souls without our being at the pains to ask for them, and will always open for us a door at which we never knock,—is, in either case, a grievous mistake. No man can pray believing prayer to be merely self-acting; and, albeit God in His mercy does often seek us when we wander from Him, yet the very Heaven-sent impulse then given seems always to be an impulse to *pray;* to return to our Father's house, and say, "I have sinned." If we neglect such inspirations, and draw no nigher to God because of them, He does nothing more. He does not force us into His arms, as He forces the planets round the sun.

I have just said that no man can pray believing Prayer to be merely self-acting. It is needful to believe that we can move another Will than our own by our supplications, before it is possible to put forth the earnest appeal of real Prayer. It will be replied, perhaps, that this statement is untrue; and that solemn, premeditated acts of resolution and aspiration are properly Prayers; even when they who use them
— bow alone
Each before the judgment throne
Of his own aweless soul;

or of an image of Buddha, or a picture of Clotilde de Vaux. But it seems to me that to give such emotions and resolutions the name of Prayers, is simply to confound two different things, just as it would be to confound a Soliloquy with a Dialogue or Address. The soliloquy may, indeed, run on the same topic as the address, and may readily be made to borrow its forms; but it is not the same thing, and to give it the same name is merely to cheat ourselves by misuse of words. To pray, as we understand the word, is to address a Person, human or divine, who is understood by him who prays actually to exist and to hear his address. To extemporize before an abstraction, *consciously recognized as such*, is not to pray. Even to address, after the Buddhist fashion, a being who, albeit he once lived upon earth, is now supposed to be unconscious of the act of his worshipper, is so far different from what we Westerns means by "Prayer," that the intelligent races who maintain such a practice see no absurdity in constructing their self-acting windmills with prayers written on their sails, to perform the barren ceremony in their stead. If there be no conscious Person to hear Prayer, there may just as well be no conscious person to pray. A machine will answer all the purposes of the case. When the Church of Rome adds a new saint to her Pantheon, the first assumption of the masses (with whom all hagiolatry begins) is, that the departed worthy has somehow come to share in the omnipresence of Deity, and can hear equally well all his worshippers scattered from

China to Peru. No one would invoke a saint who could not bend from heaven to hear the invocation.

While thus denying that moral Soliloquies made by those who believe that no God hears them, are properly Prayers, I am far from denying that they may be very sacred to him who pronounces them, or that their results on his character may be excellent. Virtue, Honour, Truth, Charity, are such blessed things, that we cannot even think of them without being the better for it, nor brush past them on our way through life without carrying away on our garments "the smell of the field which the Lord hath loved." Nay, he who truly loves these attributes of God necessarily loves Him better far assuredly than he who believes in their divine origin, but seeks not to imitate them. But with fullest admission of all this, it must remain incredible that it can be the same thing to contemplate a never-impersonated Perfection, striving unaided to approach it; and to contemplate that Perfection as embodied in a Being who hears and answers our call for help to be made holy as He is holy.

And yet, again, it may be said: If we may thus believe in the efficacy of Prayer to the Almighty, why not ask Him still, as did our fathers, to change the course of physical events; to cure sickness and stop epidemics, and send rain and sunshine and favourable winds at our option? To this I answer, that the arguments which justify Prayer for spiritual help do not apply to such cases at all; and that it seems to me incredible that Prayers for physical blessings should be granted. That God desires our spiritual good; that "His will is our salvation;" and that He has made Prayer the "means" of an immeasurable "grace;" these conclusions follow naturally and simply from the premisses of the existence of such beings as God and Man. But that God either desires, or ever actually effects, any change whatever in the order of His disposal of the forces of Nature, or that He would permit the entreaties of a thousand worlds of fallible creatures to stir Him from the course which His love and wisdom would otherwise pursue—this is not to be believed. Thus to one who regards the subject of Prayer from the point I have tried to indicate, petitions for change of weather or restoration of health, are not so much acts of piety as (if properly understood) acts of childish presumption.

But, turning from all these discussions, if we restrict ourselves solely to the conception of Prayer for God's inner action on the hearts He has made, for his help to overcome our weakness, his forgiveness to restore us after our sins, his love to fire our cold natures with Love divine and human, how inexpressibly beautiful and simple does it become! Looking at it from this point of view, we see at a glance how false and degrading are many of the common doctrines concerning it, as if it were a sort of priestly sorcery on one hand, or a commercial transaction to settle our accounts with Heaven on the other. Prayer is no artificial process invented by wise men of old to obtain a desired object from God. It is not a piece of spiritual machinery destined to bring down certain electric agencies from Heaven. It is, on the contrary, a natural act, which the Creator of the human organism must Himself have planned, and which is essentially simple, and half involuntary like the drawing of the breath. It is, in its broad sense, merely THINKING TO GOD—thinking to our invisible Divine Friend, as we all of us continually think to our dearest human friend. Our theology is our thought *of* God; our religion is our thought *to* Him. The difference between praying to God and thinking to an absent friend is only this, that we are aware the human friend knows nothing of our thoughts, while we believe that God sees them all. Thus believing, the thoughts, which commonly remain vague and formless when addressed to our absent friend (though even in his case sometimes taking the shape of audible words and imaginary letters), become naturally, when addressed to the ever-present God, more serious and definite. They are then usually embodied in language, not because any one dreams that God needs our words to know our thoughts, or imagines that Prayer can be more acceptable in such crystallized shape, but because it is our instinct always to clothe our more fervent and lucid thoughts in language as soon as they are born; and that to repress that instinct in the case of prayer to God would be to do violence to ourselves, and to lose the benefit of the definiteness and durability given to thought by such clothing.

Shall we, then, suppress this natural tendency to think to God, because we have outgrown the creeds of the past, and because we can no longer ask God for physical benefits? But *not* to think to God, *not* to speak to Him in the heart, means (so far as I can apprehend it) not to love Him, not to feel in any direct relation to Him, as our present God and Father and Master, but only to honour Him as we do some great character in history. It is almost a contradiction in terms to say we love a Living God, and yet never need to express to Him anything we are feeling, whether gratitude, or veneration, or penitence, or joy in His works. Either the Theist who refrains from prayer does so with an effort over himself, as if he refrained from any expression of love to his nearest and dearest earthly friend, or, feeling no impulse in his heart to pray, he seems to betray that he has found nothing loveable in the character of God. In the latter case, his creed, if not the Atheism of the intellect, is the Atheism of the heart. In the former, he places a constraint upon himself, not indeed unnatural in the earlier stages of the religious life, when Awe is yet stronger than Love, but which assuredly ought sooner to give way (and rarely fails to do so) under the first flood-tide of gratitude or penitence.

Having placed it in this light as the natural and fitting expression of the creature's sentiments to the Creator, it will appear perhaps somewhat harsh and legal-spirited to speak of Prayer as a Duty. And it is, in truth, a token by which we may all measure our own religious status each day or year as "under the law," or under a freer covenant, whether Prayer to us is easy, and spontaneous, or an act for whose performance a certain measure of moral force needs to be exerted. To many who have welcomed Theism as a religion of spiritual as well as intellectual freedom, without perhaps sounding it far enough to discover in how deep a region of love and union with God such freedom can alone be truly experienced, it is common to find that all statements implying that Prayer is a Duty are more or less repugnant. They seem to such persons like remnants of the fetters of an old-world slavery which has been abolished. Truly, thrice happy is he who never needs to be reminded that it is his duty to pray! But if, immersed in the interests of this life, the thoughts of Divine things grow rare and dim, and the ardour of holy ambition sinks down, and carelessness and selfishness and sin come creeping in upon each other's footsteps, is it not then a Duty—nay, the most imperative of duties—for the soul to lift itself up to its God, and cry, "Lord, save me, or I perish"? Is it not a Duty so to replenish the lamp of our spiritual life, as that such perils of darkness may never overtake us? I must confess that I believe the revolt against the doctrine of the Duty of Prayer arises, not so much from a greater sense of the rightful freedom of the spiritual affections, as from an imperfect and unreformed conception of the loveableness of Duty. To a true Theist, the idea of a firm ground of moral obligation underlying the flowery pastures of love, is no subject of regret, but of rejoicing; for, wanting it, they would be in his judgment but deceitful morasses. Duty is to him the iron frame-work within the sculptor's clay. He seeks to cover it with softer and more beautiful forms; but he knows that those sweet shapes would soon collapse and perish, were it not for the firm *armatura* beneath them. Is this a hard saying? Not so, surely, for the man for whom "Duty" means no alien law imposed by an unloved external Power, and enforced by arbitrary penalties, but the free choice of his own highest will, the voice in his heart of the God he adores, to which he joyfully gives, not so much his Obedience as his Loyalty, and to which he would strive to be faithful still, if instead of earning for him admittance into heaven, it insured his punishment in hell. To speak to such a man of an act of any kind as being an "act of Duty," is not, then, to present it to him as something naturally repulsive, or, at best, hard and stern; but, on the contrary, as something necessarily welcome, if not to his lower nature, yet inevitably to his higher self. It is practically telling him that, whether pleasant or unpleasant to his transitory wishes and the impulse of the moment, it is in accordance with the permanent desire of his heart, and his deepest consciousness of what is good and noble and beautiful in human conduct.

That Prayer is such a Duty as this for the Theist, there cannot, I conceive, exist any doubt. It is a Duty which meets us at the threshold of religion, as the staff by which our faltering steps are to be upheld and our backslidings recovered; and it is the wing on which, from the loftiest summit of morality, we must soar into the spiritual heaven of love.

But, albeit Prayer is a Duty—in a sense, the beginning and the climax of Duty—it does not follow that for the Theist there should be in it anything rigid, formal, laid down by rule and rote. The lesson taught by the originator of the High-church movement in England: "In your private prayers use the prayers of the Church," together with ordinary ecclesiastical directions to pray at stated hours and days, and in pre-arranged notes of festal gratitude or Lenten sadness—such lessons, I say, may well be given by Churches claiming Divine authority over the human intellect and conscience. But they have no sort of meaning outside their jurisdiction. For such leading-strings of the soul, it behoves every free worshipper of God to substitute such strength of aspiration, such firmness of will, as shall ensure the only point which is of spiritual importance, namely, that he lives a prayerful life. Whether he actually prays formally seven times a day, or once a week, is nothing, provided he is always ready to pray, and lovingly thinks of God and to Him, as often as in the psalm of his life that sweet key-note of all its music may fitly sound. If he feel himself weak, and lonely with that loneliness which even the firmest faith, when socially isolated, must needs endure, he may, if so it please him, make rules for himself of hours of devotion, and so supply himself with a framework in which his days may seem more safely and evenly to go on. Or he may be better pleased to make no such formal lawgiving for himself at all, and trust only to the unflagging ardour of his heart. The rule of the poet may be his rule also:

> "Keep up the fire;
> And leave the generous flames to shape themselves."

Above all, I conceive that the practice of yielding readily and joyfully to the impulses of religious feeling which at any time come to us, and the habit of filial trust enabling us freely to speak to God of all that is in our hearts, are things of infinitely more importance than the rigid adherence to any rule of devotion, however useful or reasonable it may appear.

It is frequently asked by some of the best minds of the day, Can we preserve the spirit of Religion, while relinquishing the forms in which it has hitherto been embodied? Can we keep the ennobling and purifying influences which inspired the saints and martyrs of old, while abandoning the Fountain from whence they drew them? The fear that this is impossible, and that with the disappearance of the old supernatural creed we must also witness the disappearance of all vivid personal piety, is, beyond a doubt, the mighty threat by which thousands of men and women are now scourging back their thoughts from every wandering from the fold of orthodoxy. Why is it that so many cling with the strength of desperation to dogmas against which reason and sense revolt? Why is it that others throw themselves with fanatic ardour into ritualistic practices and sacramental mysteries utterly foreign to the spirit of our age? Is it that they prefer darkness to light, difficult dogmas to obvious truths, or that they genuinely feel in the nineteenth century the reliance on religious sorcery which belonged to the Dark Ages? It were idle and unjust to think anything of the kind. They put such constraint on themselves because they consider Piety as irretrievably bound up with such beliefs and practices; and because they estimate the value of a life of personal religion as so ineffably dear, that, for its sake, no sacrifice can be too great, and they are ready to sell all they have earned or inherited of freedom and of reason, to buy this pearl of great price. The boast of the Church of Rome that she alone is the "Saint-making Church," is the one which, of all others, holds out the bribe most alluring to the purest minds of the age. They wish to be "saints." They long to preserve still and for ever the infinite treasure of a sense of personal relation to a personal God, and they cry, "Better lose reason itself than lose this life of life! Better accept all the monstrous doctrines of the creeds, and bow to all the authoritative assumptions of priests, than sink into the Secularism, the Comtism, the Atheism, which we see on all sides closing around us. Better kneel before a crucifix than bow before nothing in heaven or earth."

And which of us shall condemn these much-tried souls? Have not we also been torn asunder by our divided longings to keep close to God, and to follow that path of Truth which seemed to lead us away from Him so far? Have we not alternately stifled the cries of our intellects and our hearts, and said one hour, "Give me Truth, if it lead to the abyss!" and the next, "Sooner rob me of reason than suffer me to doubt Thee again"? We have all known somewhat of these awful strivings, at least all such amongst us who were not born heritors of liberty, but can only boast, "With a great sum—a sum of countless prayers and tears—obtained I this freedom." Need we marvel that, amid those solemn alternations, our brothers have held to the choice which seemed to be the choice of Religion itself?

Blessed be God, who has taught us at last that there are no contradictory alternations in the service of Him and of his Truth! For ever dear and sacred to us be the hour in which we learned that that path which we had followed in darkness and anguish, brought us back to the very foot of His throne! It *is* possible to preserve love and hope, and the sense of personal relation to God, all that has glorified this world and made the next seem near, after we have relinquished the creeds founded on authority. It is possible. We Theists know that it is so, and need none evermore to tell us whether we are "reconciled" with our Father on high. But if it be asked how it is that the joy and glory and hallowing influence of religion can be sustained outside the temples of old, we are compelled to answer: "By means similar to those which have always sustained them *within* the churches."

It is utterly vain to imagine that if we lose hold of faith in a Supreme Living Will, and resolve Deity into an unmoral, unintelligent Force, we can at the same time retain that sentiment for "IT" which we have given to HIM, and obtain from our ideas of such a Force the moral influences we have received from our conception of a Personal God. Least of all can it suffice (as some have fondly suggested) that we should for the future hold our religious tenets provisionally, not only as regards their form, but their substance; and remain content to suppose that the knowledge of next year, or of next century, may prove them to be altogether delusive. Rational Faith, indeed, for all coming time must be more modest than it has been in the days of authoritative revelations. It can never again say that it has reached final truth, or read the last word of God on the last leaf of his never-ended Revelations. But to *be* Faith at all, and not uttermost infidelity, it must yet say, "We shall learn *more* of

God, but we shall never learn *less* of Him. There must be a Reality somewhere in the universe which more than fulfils all our hopes, and corresponds to all our purest aspirations. When we know it, or know somewhat more of it, we shall not find it fall short of what we have believed, but infinitely surpass our highest thoughts." This alone is the faith which can ennoble humanity. To be content to suppose that when we know more, we shall believe less or love less, or perchance discover that no reality at all answers to our idea of God, is to hold our creed on terms so degrading, that no elevating influence can possibly be derived from it. Better have no religion, than a religion which we are willing to think may one day prove a gigantic delusion.

And, lastly, if Religion is still to be to mankind in the future what it has been in the past, it must still be a religion of Prayer. Nothing is changed in human nature because it has outgrown some of the errors of the past. The spiritual experience of the saintly souls of old was true and real experience, even when their intellectual creeds were full of mistakes. By the gate through which they entered the paradise of love and peace, even by that same narrow portal of Prayer, must we pass into it. No present or future discoveries in science will ever transmute the moral dross in human nature into the pure gold of virtue.

No spectrum analysis of the light of the nebulæ will enable us to find God. If we are to be made holy, we must ask the Holy One to sanctify us. If we are to know the infinite joy of Divine Love, we must seek it in Divine Communion.

CONTENTS.

PART I.

The Outer Life.

		PAGE
1.—Noon, of Day and of Life		3
2.—Morning		4
3.—Morning		5
4.—Morning		8
5.—Morning		9
6.—Morning		10
7.—Morning of a Day of Trial		12
8.—Sunset. A General Thanksgiving		13
9.—Evening		17
10.—Evening		19
11.—Evening		20
12.—Midnight		21
13.—New Year		21
14.—Sunshine		23
15.—Thanksgiving for the Love of Friends		24
16.—Thanksgiving for Friends		25

	PAGE
17.—A Mother's Prayer	27
18.—A Daughter and Mother's Prayer	28
19.—Thanksgiving for a Friend	29
20.—The Beauty of the World	30
21.—Social Pleasures	31
22.—Thanksgiving for the Lower Creatures	32
23.—Prayer for Public Good	33
24.—Work for God	37
25.—Before Work	38
26.—For one cumbered with much Serving, who seeks Rest and Refreshment with God	39
27.—Public Life	43
28.—Prière d'un Pasteur, avant de commencer sa journée de travail	44
29.—Home Trials	46
30.—A Heretic's Needs	47
31.—Intercession for a Friend	49
32.—Sorrow	50
33.—Prayer of a Mother who had lost her only Son	51
34.—Prayer in Illness	51
35.—In Suffering	53
36.—Pain and Weariness	54
37.—Restored Health	55
38.—Before Death	56

PART II.

The Inner Life.

		PAGE
1.	In the Wilderness	61
2.	On the Right Way	63
3.	Is Doubt Sin?	63
4.	God afar off	64
5.	Doubt and Faith	65
6.	Fiat Lux	68
7.	Fiat Pax	69
8.	Thanksgiving for Religious Truth	71
9.	For Faith	72
10.	The Supreme Teacher	74
11.	Why God is loved	76
12.	The Nearest One	77
13.	The Awfulness of God	78
14.	For Pardon of a Careless Life	81
15.	Sin and Sorrow	82
16.	From the Depths	83
17.	Against Thee, Thee only	84
18.	Human Love the Key of the Temple	85
19.	For Spiritual Growth	86
20.	For Strength	87
21.	For a Devoted Life	88

		PAGE
22.—Prayer of one who desires a more equal Walk with God		90
23.—Communion with God		92
24.—Thanksgiving, Spiritual and Temporal		94
25.—Living in Love, living in God		96
26.—The Mystery of Sin		98
27.—The Father of All		99
28.—Joy in God		100
29.—The World of Love		101
30.—Life with God		102
31.—Love and Serve		104
32.—See and Hear		106
33.—Here and Hereafter		107

Prayers and Thanksgivings.

Part I.

THE OUTER LIFE.

PRAYERS AND THANKSGIVINGS.

Part I.

THE OUTER LIFE.

1.

Noon, of Day and of Life.

O GOD, help me to lift my thoughts, if it be but a little way, out of the dust and smoke of life's endless battle. Let me forget for an hour my trivial cares and paltry hopes, and see all things, even the love and joy of this world, in the light of thine eternal calm.

Father, my whole existence is unworthy and imperfect. I am only half true to the law thou hast graven on my heart, half grateful or faithful to thee, my Lord. As I grow older, I cease to fall into the sins which beset me in youth, for they cease to tempt me; but I grow more engrossed with earthly interests, and less moved by the holy ambition to grow perfect as thou, my Father, art perfect. Even such repentance as I feel for my errors and shortcomings is cold and dull. I see not so much where I fail, as that my whole life is a failure. Lighten thou mine eyes, O God. Help me, for I know not how to help myself. Pour some fresh stream of love into my heart. Change this twilight of indifference into the broad lights and deep shadows of vivid spiritual life, of fervent yearning for what is good and noble and holy, and bitter loathing for all things false and selfish and vile.

2.

Morning.

ANOTHER day is before me, O Lord. Be with me, I beseech thee, during the toils and sorrows, the joys and pleasures, it may bring. Help me to carry the fragrance of thy love in my heart, so that all I do may be done to thee. Make me tread firmly on the path thy wisdom has appointed for me, not avoiding the toil or lingering for the joy. Reign thou only in my heart this day, O King; and in weal or woe, teach me to pay thee the glad tribute of prayer and praise in readier service and in deeper love.

3.

Morning.

OUR Father which art in heaven, I thank thee for the gift of life which I receive from thee afresh this morning. It is thou that hast made us, and not we ourselves, and to thee alone do we owe the renewal of our strength from day to day. Help me therefore always to feel, O Lord, that I am not my own, but thine. Grant, O my Father, that to-day I may walk steadfastly in the way of thy commandments. Create within me a loving heart of obedience. Inspire me with the childlike spirit which every moment watches for the signs of thy good pleasure, and runs to do thy holy bidding. Wherever I can trace any one of the laws that thou hast laid down, may I hasten to submit to it my selfish, restless nature; and thus may I be filled with the peace which passeth understanding, and which the world can neither give nor take away. My Father, I confess with sorrow how many times I have strayed from thy path. I am bowed down with shame in looking back on the waywardness and the rebelliousness of my past days. But claim me, I pray thee, again as thine own child. Pour into me this morning that love of thee which will bring my will into harmony with thine. Speak, Lord, and thy servant will hear. Give thou strength unto me, and I shall faithfully follow thy teaching.

And O grant unto me not only a childlike obedience, but also a childlike trust. May I rest upon thee, and depend on thy guidance through the unknown temptations and trials of the day which is now opening. Lord God! the events of the coming hours lie in thy hand. Help me always to believe that they are lovingly ordered by thee, that thou knowest and markest my path, and that again, as in the times that are gone, my strength shall be equal to my day.

My Father, I beseech thee also to fill me with right feelings towards thy other children. Make me to know in my inmost soul what it is to love my neighbour as myself. Subdue in me all selfish strivings; destroy all self-exalting aims. Melt away all the separating feelings which hinder that simple brotherhood that thou intendest for us. Lord, I lay down before thee the powers which thou hast bestowed on me, and I pray thee to use them this day through me for any work which thou willest should be done—for the good and happiness of thy children. Thankfully will I seize every occasion of kindliness, glad to be thy unworthy organ and instrument in forwarding thine all-gracious will.

Lord God, accept these my prayers, in thy great mercy. Be not far from me through the day. Uphold and comfort me with thy spiritual presence. May I obey thy holy laws, lean on thy faithful providence, and live in continual lovingness, till the evening shades have fallen, and I lie down again to rest under thy tender care. Bless me now and evermore, O my Creator and my heavenly Guide. Amen.

4.

Morning.

ALMIGHTY One, I know not how many or how few may be the morning suns which shall rise on my head ere that dawn which shall break in heaven. Let me not waste the days yet allotted to me on earth, nor stand still upon my way, for well I know that to do so is to fall back. Aid me, Father of Spirits, by thine inward grace and outward providence to gain this day some advance in holiness and nearness to thee. I know that there lies open before me even now a glorious and beautiful life, had I but resolution to lead it—a life of human kindness, in which all my words and acts should contribute to the welfare and virtue of those around me—a life of truth and courage and self-restraint, in which my evil passions should be trampled down, till I could look back on the great task of life, and say, like Christ, "It is finished!"—a life of love to thee, my God, in which my delight in thee should grow deeper and fuller year by year, till I should behold even here, and in this garb of flesh, the beginning of that eternal day of Adoration, which shall endure when all the clusters of the suns fade out and die.

O merciful God, poor and weak and sinful as I am, help me to live that blessed life, and to begin it to-day.

5.
Morning.

THROUGH the day I now begin I will strive to be perfectly true, kind, just, upright. I will try to do the work of the day with cheerfulness, to enjoy its pleasures with thankfulness, and to endure its pains (if any such come to me) with fortitude and patience. I will endeavour to render service with alacrity and unselfishness to any fellow-creature whom it may be given me to assist. I will labour to keep my heart and mind in unbroken harmony with the holy law of God.

O my Master, guide and govern me through this day, and let its close find me with a day's work faithfully done, a day's lesson thoroughly learned, a day's journey straightly travelled on the road to thee.

6.
Morning.

O DIEU, qui m'as appelé à l'existence, et qui connais mieux que moi-même mes faiblesses et mes misères, Dieu qui en me créant à ton image m'as donné tout ce qu'il faut pour te connaître et pour te servir, je t'invoque parceque tu es mon Dieu, parceque tu es le plus grand besoin de mon âme, parceque sans toi je péris comme le sarment, qui est separé du cep.

Toutes choses, O Dieu bienfaisant, vivent de toi, selon leur nature, tu rassasies à souhait toute créature vivante. Comment pourrais-je ne pas chercher à mon tour cette vie inépuisable, qui doit soutenir ma faiblesse et enricher ma pauvreté? Tu es la source infinie de la justice, de la bonté, de la vérité. Tu les offres gratuitement au cœur qui les réclame. J'en ai faim et soif, Seigneur; j'en ai besoin pour vivre, comme j'ai besoin de la lumière pour voir, et du souffle de l'air pour respirer. Elles seules peuvent donner à ma vie son caractère, sa vérité, sa beauté. Ah, que j'ouvre mon âme pour les recevoir, comme tu les donnes, sans mesure, sans réserve, fidèle à la sanctification qu'elles exigent de moi, fidèle aussi à en demander chaque jour davantage ! Je les cherche à ce moment de la prière, où mon âme s'entretient, avec toi, comme l'enfant avec son père ; mais je veux les avoir avec moi pendant tout le cours de cette journée. Qu'elles m'accompagnent dans mes travaux, dans toutes mes relations avec mes semblables, dans mes joies comme dans mes peines ; qu'elles soient la lampe de mes pieds, la lumière de mon sentier, l'inspiration de ma vie entière.

O mon Dieu, il est vrai que mon passé pèse sur moi d'une manière qui souvent m'attriste et souvent me décourage. Que de fautes n'ai-je pas commises ! Que de devoirs n'ai-je pas négligés ! Combien de fois l'égoisme, la vie des sens, l'orgueil, n'ont ils pas triomphé chez moi, des inspirations de ton Esprit, de cet Esprit qui m'appelle sans cesse à l'amour, à l'humilité, au sacrifice. Hélas, en me connaissant, comme je me connais, combien de fois succomberai-je encore à la tentation !

Toutefois, Seigneur, il y a pardon par devers toi, afin que tu sois craint. Subviens à ma faiblesse. Que ces fautes même que je déplore, servent à ma sanctification en me faisant rechercher ta communion avec plus d'ardeur.

Père saint, m'approcher de toi, c'est tout mon bien, c'est aussi le bien de tous mes frères. Que nous répondions tous aux appels de ta bonté, pour nous réchauffer aux rayons du Soleil de la justice. Au lieu de vivre loin de toi, séparés les uns des autres, que nous recherchions de bien près tes saintes influences, afin que réunis en toi, nous vivions tous pour glorifier ton nom, pour te servir jusqu'à notre mort, et au delà de la tombe dans la vie éternelle. Qu' ainsi se réalise cette prière, qui résume toutes les autres, et que je t'addresse dans la communion de l'église universelle, "Notre Père, qui es aux cieux, que ton règne vienne." Amen.

7.

Morning of a Day of Trial.

O FATHER, aid me this day to use the power, which surely thou hast not failed to give me, to overcome its special temptations. I see before me the danger that I may fail, that I may give way on the occasion when . . . .

I will *not* fail, O Lord! In thy strength I resolve to do what I know thou wouldst have me do. Help, O help me to keep my resolution sacredly, even as I make it solemnly at thy feet.

8.

Sunset. A General Thanksgiving.

IN this calm, beautiful hour, the Sabbath hour of the day, I turn to thee, my Father, the Lord of Peace, the Giver of Rest, the Author of all things beautiful and good. Thou needest not my thanks, O bounteous God; but my soul needs to rehearse thy blessings and to praise thine infinite loving-kindness.

While the twilight fades in the west, and the birds nestle in the branches, and the hush of the night wind passes over the sleeping woods, and the stars come out in the sky, I would enter like a worshipper into this thy holy temple of nature, and lift to thee, O Lord of All, the orison of my humble praise.

I bless thee, O God, for the life thou hast given me; for the great boon of existence in the universe of which thou art King:
I bless thee, O my God.

For such measure of health and strength as I possess, for hearing and sight, for food and clothing and abode and sleep:
I bless thee, O my God.

I bless thee for the friends yet near me, and for the dear ones who have gone home to thee; for their tender love, and for the happy power to love and honour them in return:
I bless thee, O my God.

For the nearest and dearest friend of all; for the joy of that love which thou alone hast fully known and understood:
I bless thee, O my God.

For the power to relieve the wants of others, to mitigate some of their sorrows, and right a portion of their wrongs:
I bless thee, O my God.

I bless thee that thy mercies are not for me alone, but are spread over all thy creatures, and that there are thousands who possess joys which are denied to me, and happiness which I shall never share:

I bless thee, O my God.

I bless thee for the order of thy beautiful world; for sun and moon, and stars and sea; for clouds and mountains, and running waters:

I bless thee, O my God.

For the fruits of the summer and the autumn's store, for winter's frost and the ever-renewing miracle of spring; for brilliant day, and holy night, and soft sweet twilight:

I bless thee, O my God.

For the stately trees of the forest, and for the flowers which bloom over all the earth like tokens to show that thy love is everywhere:

I bless thee, O my God.

For the sweet-singing birds, and the loving and faithful brutes whom thou hast made our humble friends; for all the creatures which fill earth and air and sea with their innocent happiness:

I bless thee, O my God.

I bless thee for the special gifts thou hast

given to the race of man; for speech and writing, whereby the souls of the living and the dead commune together; for science and art and poetry:

I bless thee, O my God.

For the inspiration wherewith thou hast enlightened all the good and wise of every age and clime, and which thou didst pour in fullest measure through the soul of Christ when he learned to call thee Father:

I bless thee, O my God.

For the blissful throb of gladness when I have obeyed thy voice of Conscience; for the joyless void when I have been deaf to its mandates; for the bitter anguish of remorse when I have defied and disobeyed it:

I bless thee, O my God.

For every joy which brought me to thy feet in gratitude; for every pang which taught me the loathsomeness of sin:

I bless thee, O my God.

For thy myriad gifts I bless thee! But above all others, for this—that thou hast taught

me to know thee, and that I can trace thy blessed hand in all things good and beautiful:
I bless thee, O my God.

I bless thee that I know thou lovest all the millions of thy creatures who fill the stars with their joy and with thy glory.:
I bless thee, O my God.

I bless thee for the dearest of all gifts of time or of eternity. I bless thee that with my mind I know, and with my heart I feel, that thou my God art good:
I bless thee, O my God.

9.

Evening.

LORD of heaven and earth, another of the days which thou hast allotted to me is past and spent, and again I am going to be refreshed with sleep. I thank thee, O my Father, for the many mercies which I have received from thee since this morning. Thy loving-kindness is constant and infinite. Thou hast guarded me to-day from dangers, and strengthened me in weakness. Thou hast led me with kind and fatherly guidance, and thou hast made me glad with unnumbered gifts and favours. I pray thee to forgive the faithlessness which thine all-seeing eye has discerned in my heart this day. Pardon the selfishness, the pride, the disobedience, that have spoiled and disfigured the precious minutes and hours which have been entrusted to me by thee. O my God, I would return to thee with the penitence of a sorrowing child; and I beseech thee to grant that my future days may be spent more fully in thy blessed service.

Let thy peace rest upon my soul this night. I lay myself down under the shelter of thy loving care. Prepare me either to wake again for a longer term of life in this world, or to obey a summons into thy more immediate presence. Anew I surrender myself to thee. Thou art my Lord and the Source of my being. Watch over me and bless me, and bless all those whom I love, and let them also rest in thy holy keeping this night. Amen.

10.
Evening.

TO thee, O God, I pray, thou who art ever present, and knowest all we want or should have. Help me to submit now and at all times to thy will, knowing it must be right. Direct my mind to lead those I should influence into the right path, with love and gentleness and firmness. Govern my thoughts, which are often rambling and desultory, and need calmness. Give me toleration to the differing minds of others, even though to me the right and the wrong are clear. Thou alone knowest whence and wherefore our influences are derived. That thou art good, all Nature testifies; and the happiness which invariably attends all self-denying efforts to contribute to the happiness of others, is a blessing which surely springs in our hearts directly from thee. As we lay down each night to sleep, trusting implicitly to thy merciful care of us, so may we when death comes resign ourselves to the same loving protection, and feel sure we are safe. Fill our hearts with gratitude to thee, and thus make us at all times aware of thy presence, thy mercy and thy love.

11.

Evening.

O GOD, as the sun goes down upon another day, I thank thee for the light and warmth which clothe thy world with glory; for the quiet night now closing around me, and for all that makes life so beautiful.

O holy Father, I am not worthy of all thy goodness. The service I have this day rendered unto thee has been cold and negligent; I have served thee as a hireling, and not with the gladness of a son; and so the thought of thy presence has not dwelt in my heart to hallow all my day. Yet thou hast been with me, O God; thou hast helped me sometimes to choose good and to resist evil; thou hast kept great temptations away from me, and hast made me glad with the love and sympathy and beauty of thy creatures. Be with me through this night, and help me to serve thee henceforward with a holier zeal; that so, when the last long night comes, I may be prepared, by the faithful performance of the work thou hast given me here, for the more glorious service of the life to come.

12.

Midnight.

I ARISE from the blessed sleep thou givest, to thank thee for thy goodness to me and to all thy creatures. I love thee, Holiest of the Holy, Best of the Good! O, for thy dear love's sake, make me to love thee more.

13.

New Year.

O ETERNAL and Holy Father, now on the eve of a new year my heart goes up to thee in thankfulness which I have no voice to utter, no words to express.

O thou who hast hedged me round with so many evidences of thy love, I would fain render unto thee the thank-offering of grateful service for all the many gifts by which thou hast revealed thyself unto me.

I bless thee for the friends whom thou hast given me, and for the love which in them thou hast revealed unto me; for all thy gifts of speech, of art, of science, by which thou hast taught me to lift my heart in thankfulness to thee, and to share with others the treasures of thy love. And, above all, I offer unto thee humble and hearty praise for the knowledge which thou hast in thine infinite goodness added unto me, that it is from thy fatherly hand all good gifts come, not to me only, but to all thy children everywhere. Be with me in the coming year, O my Father, as thou hast ever been, and make me, I pray thee, more worthy of the countless mercies which I have received at thy hands. Make me more humble, more diligent, more ready to listen to thy voice within me. Let not my sins get the better of me. Let me not lose the consciousness of thy love, nor cease to feel how terrible is thy displeasure. Save me not from the consequences of my faults, but, if it be possible, O Lord, let them not bring evil upon others. Visit, I beseech thee, with thy chastisement all my sins, negligences and ignorances, and give me true repentance. Make my future life a constant thank-offering to thee, and teach me to find my greatest joy in the service thy wisdom appoints for me, whatever that service may be. Thus, when all the years of my life are told, I may still bless thee, "who hast redeemed my life from destruction, and crowned me with loving-kindness and tender mercies."

14.

Sunshine.

FATHER, I am happy. I long to thank thee for my happiness, for thou hast given it to me, O thou great, ineffable God! It is thy world in which I live and rejoice, thy laws of nature and of human love which bring me joy. Thine endless, awful felicity can only consist in pouring down the rain of blessings through all thy worlds for ever; and amidst them all, I, even I, have been given my portion and have not been forgotten. I thank thee, I bless thee, O gracious, kind and merciful Lord. Henceforth I will strive to make my life one long sweet psalm of thanksgiving. When trouble and care come back to me, I will remember how the world looks to me to-day. I will strive to be good and merciful and forgiving to thy creatures, even as thou, blessed God in heaven, hast been good and merciful and all-forgiving to me.

15.

Thanksgiving for the Love of Friends.

MY heart is very full, O Lord; I would come to thy feet and speak to thee. My Father, I thank thee for the kindness of thy children to me, for their kindness so much greater than I deserve—I, so often weak and selfish. How blessed has my life been made by their kind words, their loving and tender actions! Sometimes I have toiled long alone, and have grown sad and heavy-hearted, and then, even then, a child of thine will speak to me a word of love most truly divine, and the whole long day when that word was spoken will be perfumed with sweetest odours, and my faith will grow firm in love and goodness and all possibilities of nobleness, and I shall have hope and heart, and a spirit renewed within me.

I thank thee, O dear Lord, that thou breathest

such love upon us, that men may so speak and act, and be angels from thee to each other. I know that their love is from thee; they can love because thou art loving.

16.

Thanksgiving for Friends.

FATHER of the family of earth and heaven, I thank thee for the great share thou hast given to me of the joy of human affection. Hadst thou made me the inheritor of millions of gold and silver, and yet allowed no true heart to love me, and denied to me the power of unselfish love, then were I a poor beggar in comparison of what I am now. Thou hast given me friends worthy of my honour and my tenderness; thou hast permitted them to see me, faulty as I am, with kindly eyes of love; and thou hast not left my heart so cold, but that I can recognize their goodness, and glory in their gifts, and love them tenderly and faithfully. Bless thou these friends whose souls thou hast knit with mine, O merciful Father, with all the riches of thy light and grace. Give to them the strength they need to overcome whatsoever temptations beset them. Take from them earthly care and anxiety, and teach them to rest their hearts on thee. Comfort them in sorrow and pain, and make their path through life and death like the light which shineth more and more unto the perfect day. And, O my God, while I love them and bless thee for their love, help me to be worthy of them, and to imitate the virtues for which I give them honour. Make their patience, their courage, their faith, their benevolence, their piety and their unselfishness, the rebuke of my failings. When I am discontented, let me think of ——; when faithless, of ——; when resentful, of ——; when selfishly thinking of myself alone, of ——. So make me at last not unfit to join these dear ones, and the blessed band of all the good and wise, in that world which lies beyond the gates of death, where we shall all look into one another's inmost hearts, and know even as we are known.

17.

A Mother's Prayer.

O GOD, our loving Father, hear me, and strengthen me, as I pour forth my prayers to thee. I thank thee for the great blessings thou hast granted me; pardon my faults, in not bravely acting up to duty, and allowing the small trials of life to govern me. I thank thee for all the goodness thou hast given me in those I love. Guide me in my daily conduct, and give me a judicious spirit in the training of my children. Love to them thou hast implanted in me, and in the knowledge of this I rely on thine infinite love; full of justice, yet full of tender mercy. When depression comes, let my thoughts fly to thee and thy everlasting goodness, as that alone can comfort me; and with the outward expression of thankfulness for thy mercies, strengthen my sense of them. Keep up in me an honest truthfulness (a great need in the conflict of this life), a charity towards others, and a cheerful spirit, which is the proof of a thankful one. Of those dear ones who have left us, I have blessed memories;

and as I feel their spirits are ever with us, may I act as they would have wished on earth, and as I feel their loving spirits now wish. May we meet in the great hereafter! What it is, we know not; but thou art good, and as thou carest for us here, we shall ever be in the same merciful hands.

18.

A Daughter and Mother's Prayer.

MY Father, my Father! In that name is my hope and my comfort. When I whisper it to myself I dare to feel that I inherit life from thee, that life which, inspiring my thought and love to forget the boundaries that press on my senses, teaches me to own them immortal. O, faint image of thy love and thy thought! but a child can dimly understand its Father's mind.

My Father and my father's Father! As I remember thy spirit that I have seen in him, as I feel his spirit living still in me, I tremble and I rejoice as I recognize thy presence that accompanies his in my heart. O divine consolation, to know that there is no real separation!

My Father, and the Father of my child! In his dawning smile I see the brightness of thy love smile upon me. Help me so to live before him, that no influence from my relationship may weaken the ties of higher kindred that unite him to thee.

O my Father, the thought of thee is my rest; help me to make it also my activity.

19.

Thanksgiving for a Friend.

BLESSED Father, I thank thee that thou hast given me the dearest of all earthly gifts, a beloved and loving friend. I thank thee that in thy providence thou hast brought us together and enabled us to see one another's souls; and I thank thee that thou hast given to us the gift, better than all the gifts of genius, the blessed power of love. O God, make that love, which is thy gift, and which has been born in thy presence, and nourished by communion of sacred thoughts, make it altogether noble and holy, so that our bond to one another may be a bond of self-sacrifice and generosity. Teach us the lesson of that worthiest friendship which seeks the virtue even more than the happiness of the one beloved, and grieves over moral failure more than over pain and sorrow, and joys in every brave and unselfish action more than in the pleasure and prosperity of our friend. O God, our hearts are weak and fond, and cannot yet soar to such love divine; but aid us, by faithful counsels and true acts of holy friendship, to climb towards it step by step. Make us grateful to thee always for the infinite joy of our love, and let us live and die near to thee, and awake to be for ever with thee and with one another.

20.

The Beauty of the World.

FATHER, I bless thee that thou hast given me this day the pure delight of beholding the beauties of thy creation. For the sight of the hills and streams and woods and skies, I thank thee, bountiful **Lord**. Thou hast suffered me to share in thine eternal joy in all things beautiful. Thou art my Father; and it is with the sympathy of an adoring child that I behold the works of thy hands.

21.

Social Pleasures.

KIND and merciful God, numberless are the pleasures thou givest me day by day. Especially I thank thee now for the varied delights of heart and intellect which come to me through the society of the good and gifted men and women with whom it is my happy lot to associate. For the keen enjoyment of their conversation, full of wise, fresh thoughts, and delicate tenderness, and bright imaginations, and manifold wealth of allusions and memories, I would thank thee, my Maker, as I thank thee for the fruits and flowers which bring delight to my bodily senses. For playful mirth and jest, and that ever-renewed pleasure, spread over half my life, which has its source in the love of wit and humour, for these also I bless thee, thou who hast made the birds to sing, and the young brutes to play, and the winds and waves to laugh in the sunshine. I fear not to laugh in thy presence, Father in Heaven, more than in infancy I feared to play beneath my mother's eye. Thou hast given to me this innocent joy, like all else that my nature possesses; and well I know that for thy child, O all-good One, to enjoy is to obey. Only help me to remember thee always, amid heartiest mirth or engaged in the most engrossing converse. Thus my laughter will never pain or hurt any creature of thine, and my words will betray no principle to which in calmer hours I have vowed to be faithful.

22.

Thanksgiving for the Lower Creatures.

BOUNTIFUL Lord, thy world seems filled this summer morning with life and enjoyment. The stately beasts browsing in the rich pastures, the lark singing far away out of sight in the blue sky, the fish darting and leaping in the stream, the bees murmuring among the blossoms of the hawthorn—all are filled with as much happiness as their natures can bear. Their little cups are full. And my heart, O God, is full also. I love thee, I thank thee, blessed Lord of all, for thy kindness to these thy creatures who know not the hand which feeds them. To me thou hast given a mind to seek and find thee, a heart to adore thee, a voice to speak thy praise. I am the only priest in this thy temple of the fields and woods, and for all the humble ones around I speak the glad Te Deum.

23.

Prayer for Public Good.

FATHER, with the prophets of old, I would rejoice in the glories of thy visible creation, and bless thee that thou hast given me eyes to see and a heart to feel the beauty of thy works. Yet how often I pass them by unheeded! They lie before me like an open book, but I turn away from its pages to fix my gaze on the dusty highway of life, with its vain shows and sordid traffic; their silent calmness encompasses me day and night, but I break the stillness to crowd my hours with unworthy anxieties, feverish hopes and fruitless vexations. Too often I convert my happiest duties into tasks, and sow the seed of pain in my dearest affections.

Father, suffer me not to turn this beautiful world of thine into a weary wilderness, thick set with thorns of my own planting, against which my perverse heart presses itself in vain. Give me courage to pluck up by the roots the prickly briars of vanity, self-will, and over-anxious care. Let me walk with free steps in the field of duty thou hast assigned to me. Grant that my strength may be spent upon the fruitful work that thou hast set before me, not wasted on the weary taskings of my own self-love; that my endurance may be reserved for the trials thou dost send me, not consumed by those I fashion for myself. Let not the powers and emotions thou hast given me be absorbed in a ceaseless round of inward struggle. Lift me out of myself; give me insight into the life of others, and a true heart to feel for them, that I may work for them in a spirit of respectful sympathy, not of self-satisfied benevolence. Shew me, O Lord, the right path through the difficulties that beset their course and mine, and grant me strength to enter upon it fearlessly, notwithstanding all worldly obstacles, and patient steadiness to pursue it to the end. May no fear of man or men's opinions hold me back, or make me turn aside into an easier road.

Father of all the families of the earth, thou who hast ordered the races and nations of men, and hast given to each its appointed work, I pray thee to shew us as a people what thou wouldest have us to do. Enlighten our minds to discern thine eternal laws standing steadfast and unchanged amidst the dark storms of human passion and the surging strife of human wills. Let us not believe that the revenge and hate and envy and selfish ambition that are sins in individuals, can be guiltless in nations. O God, who hast created men in thine own image, and placed them here that they should love each other and work together as brothers for the common good, help us to see how truth and right are to be upheld by true and right and loving means; how justice and freedom are to be secured by just and noble acts. Our hearts fail us at the spectacle of mutual destruction; at the sight of the crushing misery, the savage waste, the fierce passions and fiercer callousness, the deep and wide-spreading moral mischiefs of war. O pity the sufferers, assuage their bitter pain and griefs; strengthen the self-devoted, succour the tempted, purify the evil; let not all the woe be fruitless. Father, in the presence of such misery and confusion, such clashing of mutual rights and mutual wrongs, I know not what to ask; I can only look up to thee; thou alone canst guide our course aright; only in thy holy providence, which is ever working to bring good out of evil, can I find a resting-place for hope.

And if to ourselves troubled times should come, and our long prosperity be for a while suspended, grant that adversity and struggle may quicken us to learn thy lessons. Let the need of action rouse us from our apathetic acquiescence in existing evils; let the need of endurance brace our powers and raise our hope;

let the fire of national trial burn up the overgrowth of our luxury, melt away our class-selfishness, fuse our cold hard prudence into a clear-sighted and self-forgetful energy, and make our whole people glow with a common faith in the Right and trust in thee. Thy holy will, O God, is the law of Right for nations as for individual men; teach us as a people to see it more clearly, to follow it more ardently, to guide our whole course by it more steadfastly and unswervingly; so shall our hearts be filled with thankful hope for the future of our country, while we strive ever more faithfully and fearlessly to do thy work in the present. Amen.

24.

Work for God.

O LORD, keep my heart pure. Strengthen in me that which makes me thy child, stamped with thine image, the will to choose good and reject evil, the love of righteousness and hatred of iniquity, the tender, self-forgetting love of my fellow-creatures, thy other children. O make me single-minded, steady through good report and evil report in the task I have undertaken, caring nothing for self-glorification, but only to do as perfectly as I can the work my hand findeth to do. Let me rise each morning saying with my whole heart and mind and strength: Lo, I come to do thy will, O God! Let me bear the pain and sorrows and failures of my life, as the blows and wounds the soldier must meet in battle, content to know that I fall doing my duty, and that thy purpose cannot fail. Be my stay and guide through the burden and heat of the day, that I may be able each night, as I lie down to rest, to say: "I have done this day the work thou gavest me to do;" and to feel that my labour has not been in vain, since it tended to make thy will be done on earth as it is in heaven. And when the last night cometh, grant to me, O Father, the supreme joy of saying with him who shewed us this way, even though, like him, I say it from the cross: "It is finished."

25.

Before Work.

MERCIFUL God, I return to my daily task. Let me perform it with the sense that thou overseest both what I do and why I do it. Give me the comfort hereafter, when my last day's work is done, to feel I have never written a falsehood, or supported an injustice, or wounded an innocent fellow-creature. And O, if it be possible, give even to me, unworthy that I am, the glory and the joy of having in my lifetime struck some blows which shall not have fallen wholly in vain in the battle for the Right and the True.

26.

For one cumbered with much serving, who seeks rest and refreshment with God.

O THOU, who never restest or hastest, but art the energy of all force, the source of all order, the spring of all life, by thee all things move quietly in their appointed courses, and the universe stands fast evermore. And I, too, would fain work with thee in my allotted place, and according to the strength which thou hast given me. I earnestly desire to be able to consecrate to thee, with increasing sincerity and completeness, all my powers and my whole life. But I cannot attain to any peaceful and equable energy; my heart is perplexed and divided, even when it most eagerly desires to be wholly thine. It is not, O Father, that I am cumbered with the weaknesses of the flesh and the cares of this life, for these are the necessary conditions of my service, and thou wilt help me to make them the occasions of my strength. But even when I have risen to the height of a sincere aspiration after dutifulness, and have girded myself for toil in thy vineyard, other difficulties perplex, other temptations assail me, and I find not the peace which I had hoped. I am divided between conflicting duties; and it is hard for me to know that I am serving thee where thou wouldst have me work. My toil goes away from me, and comes not back again. Thy ways, O God, are slow, thy winters long and drear; and because I see no springing furrows, I am tempted to believe that there will be no harvest. I have striven to enter into communion with thee by labour, and now I long for the restfulness of meditation and of prayer; while I work, I am too much with myself and with men, and I would live more and more quietly with thee, and grow into the likeness of thy holiness, and go down no more into the fields of effort till I can render thee a better and less incomplete obedience. And yet the night cometh, and I must work while it is day. I am in a strait betwixt two. Where shall I find thee, O God, my strength, my rest?

O Father, take me more completely out of myself and make me thine. For it is not my own work that I try to do, but thine. Thou needest not me, nor any son of man; and as the years come and go, and the generations pass, thou workest still thy wise designs. Make me feel that to try, with all my heart and strength, to do my duty, is indeed to have done it; and that for all the errors and shortcomings of thy children who in truth endeavour to do thy work, thy might and wisdom will far more than make up. Give me a steadier and more cheerful faith that no honest labour for thee is ever in vain, but, near or far off, earns its just reward. Strengthen me to apply myself earnestly to the duty that lies nearest to my hand, and to think no service mean which I can perform in the recollection of thy holiness, and in the consciousness of working together with thy will. And make me feel, as in my better moments I have felt before, that I need not lie still to see thee, or be girt about with the silence of meditation to hear thee; but that thou art never nearer to thy servants than in the throng and press of daily duty, and speakest to them from the midst of common cares and temptations. Give me always an eye to see thee, an ear to catch thy voice, a heart to love thy will, and, working or resting, I shall need no more. And from the earthly toil which makes rest sweet and needful, lift my heart and hope to the heavenly labour which is rest itself; and quicken me into communion with thine own everlasting energy, which is eternal joy.

Public Life.

O GOD, I find it very hard to bring my inward and my outward, my private and my public life into harmony. When I go forth into the world, if I do not forget and am not wholly faithless to the conceptions of duty I have recognized in thy nearer presence, yet I am sensible that lower and more selfish motives, and laxer principles as regards justice and truth, sway me more than they ought to do. Alone with thee, I acknowledge no law but thy sacred voice. In the crowd, the laws of expediency and conformity with the common standard, have power over me. O God, help me to greater consistency in this matter, for else is my loyalty to thee nought but self-delusion. Whenever I exercise any power, let the remembrance that thou, God, art my Judge and my Master be ever present with me. Never let influence of mine be given to an ignoble cause or from an unworthy motive. Help me to keep my honour clear and stainless, not only as the world may count honour, but as I count it myself, in perfect integrity and purity and simplicity. O God, even though I live in a crowd, keep me, I pray thee, unspotted from the world.

28.

Prière d'un Pasteur, avant de commencer sa journée de travail.

MON Dieu, j'ai à te rendre grâces des dons si nombreux de ta Providence paternelle, pour ce repos de la nuit, qui a réparé mes forces, pour le pain quotidien que ta bonté nous dispense, pour la joie que nous avons eue de prendre en famille, le repas du matin. Que te rendrai-je, O Eternel, pour tous ces bienfaits qui se renouvellent chaque jour? Je prendrai la coupe des délivrances, et je bénirai le nom de l'Eternel. Que mon âme, Seigneur, n'oublie aucun de tes bienfaits, que ces témoignages de ta bonté mettent sur mes lèvres le psaume de la reconnaissance, et dans mon cœur la firme résolution de te servir à jamais.

Me voici sur le point de commencer ma journée de travail. O mon Dieu, puisque c'est mon

heureuse tâche de parler de toi à mes frères.
Donne-moi d'être, le premier, tellement pénétré
de vérité, que je puisse aussi les conduire en toute
vérité. Que leur prospérité spirituelle soit pour
moi l'objet d'une pressante sollicitude. Je voudrais apprendre à les aimer comme tu les aimes,
toi-même, en cherchant avec eux et pour eux
ce qui doit faire notre bien commun, ce qui
est pour nous tous la seule chose nécessaire.
Quand je dois parler en ton nom à ton peuple
assemblé pour le culte public, que je le fasse
dans l'esprit qui convient à ce ministère sacré.
Garde-moi du malheur et du péché de donner
à ma prédication une préparation insuffisante,
mais qu'elle témoigne toujours de l'onction et
de la puissance que l'on trouve auprès de toi,
par la communion de ton Esprit.

Dans mes relations de chaque jour avec mes
paroissiens, donne-moi cette sagesse, cet amour
des âmes, et ce zèle, qui rendront mon ministère utile. Que je puisse donner à chacun
la parole qui convient à son état ; à l'affligé,
la consolation ; à celui qui est dans la joie,
un appel à la reconnaissance ; les choses éternelles à ceux qui les oublient, la confiance à

ceux qui désespèrent, l'amour du prochain à ceux qui vivent dans l'égoisme. Je voudrais, O mon Dieu et mon Père, vivre, et me pénétrer tellement des choses invisibles, que ma seule présence fût par elle-même une prédication. Pour faire du bien, donne-moi d'être bon; pour nourrir la piété des autres, donne-moi de chercher auprès de toi, la nourriture de la vie éternelle. Donne-moi, Seigneur, l'esprit des grands hommes de ton église, cet esprit de foi, de renoncement et d'amour, qui fait les serviteurs fidèles; et bénis l'œuvre de mes mains. Qui, O mon Dieu, bénis l'œuvre des mes mains dans cette journée, et dans toutes celles qui suivront. Amen.

29.
Home Trials.

ALMIGHTY and Holy Father, I am going back to a life that has always been fraught with temptations for me; and though I know that those which will beset me spring chiefly out of the foolish vanity of my own heart, yet of myself alone I shall fail to resist them, as I have so often done before. Therefore, O God, I claim thy Fatherly succour. Help me to cast my foolishness away. Teach me not to scorn those things which irritate me. They are small and paltry, but they are strong and mighty to overthrow me. Teach me to restrain the cutting answer, the sharp retort, that are so pleasant for one short moment to make, so bitter to remember afterwards. Help me, O Lord, to think of thee when I am tempted. Take not away the temptation from me, but for thy pity's sake make me strong to stand against it; to bear the taunt and yet keep silence unto thee, to be stanch and true to thee and to the faith I so unworthily profess. Teach me in each temptation to see a chance of proving that my love to thee is no vain delusion. Hold me up, O God, for I cannot stand alone.

30.

A Heretic's Needs.

GIVE me light and strength, I pray thee, O God, to walk unflinchingly in the difficult path of honesty and charity. Severed as I am by religious differences from those nearest to me in the world, teach me alike to be true to my own convictions and to spare them every needless pang. Make me bear cheerfully those seeming withdrawals of confidence and affection, those misconceptions of my motives and conduct, which are inevitable in our relative positions, and let me trust to the kindness and justice which I know lie at the bottom of the hearts so dear to me, to vindicate me at last. Let me keep always in mind the fact, that the mere knowledge that I do not share their most cherished beliefs is a source of endless uneasiness to my friends, and that it is my part to atone in every way possible for such trouble. Forgive me, O God, I pray thee, for the many times in which I have failed in this duty, and bless —— and —— a thousand-fold; and forgive us all if in such straits the law of kindness be not always inviolate amongst us. But, O God, give me not only patience and wisdom, but also firmness and courage to resist the frequent temptation to seem to yield where I ought not to yield, and to keep silence when truthfulness demands that I shall speak. How shall I ask thee to lead me yet further and into still higher truth, if I shrink from confessing to all men the truths thou hast taught me already? Master and Lord, make me honest before all things; then make me patient and loving.

31.

Intercession for a Friend.

O GOD, one whom I love is in bitter grief; help and comfort *him*, I beseech thee. I know thy love for *him* is infinitely greater and tenderer than mine, and I presume not to dictate unto thee how thou shouldst comfort *him*. But, my Father, if I were in sorrow myself I should come to thee, and so I bring thee confidently the sorrow of my friend. Open thou *his* heart, O God, to receive thy holy love. Pour down upon *him* the comfort which only thou canst give, and lead *him* to rest under the shadow of thy Almighty wings. Help me, I pray thee, to love *him* better; give me wisdom and deep sympathy to understand *his* sorrow, and teach me to bear true witness of thee.

O Holy and All-loving Father, I know thy great mercy and love are over all. Help me to trust thee in all things, for those I love as well as for myself; and help me to remember that what thou dost is right, and that my wisdom is but foolishness before thee.

32.

Sorrow.

O GOD, thou hast struck me very heavily. Thou hast taken from me all the joy of life. Nothing remains of happiness for me in this world, only an aching void where once were love and delight. I am alone, and have none to whom to turn in my desolation. If it were blind Fate which had thus torn from me the joy of my heart, the light of my eyes, I could not bear it. I would end my misery and lie down in the grave where my beloved one is sleeping. But it is not Fate, nor unmeaning, unintelligent Law. It is thou, O awful God, who hast done it. In thine absolute Justice thou hast smitten me. It is only I who suffer.

My darling has gone home to thee, and is at rest.

God, I submit! Break my guilty heart, if so thou willest. I would not have thy justice turn aside because I lie in its path. My earthly love is over. O Father in heaven, help me to say, "I still love thee."

33.

Prayer of a Mother who had lost her only Son.

O GOD, whose righteous will it was to afflict me with the severest of all human sorrows, give me power in my anguish still to trust in thy goodness. Teach me still to say, truly and fervently: "I thank thee, O Lord, that thou hast taken my angel from every ill and every suffering, and placed him safe in thine eternal bosom."

34.

Prayer in Illness.

MY God, my Father, thou who through all my life hast listened when my heart cried after thee, thou who in the days of my childhood dealt so tenderly with me, and in later years hast ever deigned to hear me in times of sorrow or of joy: O hear me now, even now, in this hour of weariness and distress, when my spirit faints in the weakness of the flesh, and my soul is dull with fear.

O Father, thou alone knowest all the folly and weakness which beset me; thou alone seest all the mean desires which throng my unsatisfied heart. I long for powers which may not be mine. I crave for work which I may hardly perform. I grasp at happiness which thou withholdest from me. I fall into faithlessness and sin. Yet, O gracious Father, speak to me again. Let me feel once more thy blessed presence in my breast; and these privations, which seem so grievous now, will be as chains to draw me closer to thyself. Thy might shall help my helplessnesss; thy love shall cover all my loneliness; thy peace shall turn my unrest to calm. My God, now let me rest in thee; and in thy strength I shall be strong.

35.

In Suffering.

RETIENS sur mes lèvres, O Dieu tout puissant, et refoule dans mon cœur toute plainte et tout murmure. Ne sais tu pas que je souffre, et n'est tu pas le Dieu souverainement sage, qui ne permet pas que rien se fasse au hasard, qui ne laisses pas même un passereau tomber par terre sans savoir dans quel bût?

Tu as décidé que nul être ne passerait de la naissance à la mort sans souffrir. Tu as préparé pour chacun de tes enfans une coupe amère. Tu veux que je boive la coupe de mes souffrances. Eh bien, mon Dieu et mon Père, je prends cette calice, je la bois, et je la bénisse.

O merci, grand Dieu! Dejà je sens la certitude de la paix calmer le trouble qui m'agite. Je suis en ce moment non malheureux, mais heureux, non à plaindre, mais à féliciter, car tu es proche, O Dieu, tout puissant et tout bon, et tu as préparé la baume pour guérir mes blessures, et la consolation pour relever mon cœur.

36.

Pain and Weariness.

O GOD, in my weakness I come to thee, and pray thee of thy Fatherly love and tenderness to have pity upon me. I am crushed down with pain and weariness, and only the sense of thy presence sustains me. My God, it is thee, thee only, that I love, not only when thou loadest me with gladness, but now and always. Give me patience to endure this pain which thou seest fit that I should suffer, that so it may be sanctified unto me, and I may find in it the blessing which all thy gifts contain. Thou knowest, O Father, how frail I am, and how my thoughts are distracted and turned away from thee who art my strength, so that for very weariness I cannot pray. Thou seest my heart. Thou knowest that, though words fail me, I do long to be brave and patient. O give me loving faith to lift my heart to thee, away from this earthly pain; make me strong in the certainty that it is from thee, and that all thy gifts are good. Help me to remember that it is not enough to say, "Thy will be done," without hearty effort to know what thy will is, and to accomplish it. Give me patient faith to use the means of recovery which thou shalt send. Only, O God, let not this cloud of pain hide thee from me; let not my soul be numb to thy dear arms around me; so, in spite of weariness and suffering, thy holy Presence shall make me glad, until thou shalt send me the sleep of death, and take me home to thee.

37.

Restored Health.

FATHER in Heaven, I thank thee for the health thou hast restored to me. Teach me, I humbly beseech thee, to use it in thy most blessed service. Thou hast been with me in sickness and in sorrow; and in bitter sin thou didst not forsake me. Be with me still, O holy and merciful God, in health and joy. It is hard sometimes to remember thee, when the multitudinous occupations of returning health crowd about me, or when strength fails me and I long for the quiet life I led with thee in sickness.

Be with me, then, lest on one hand I grieve foolishly over mere weakness as sin, or on the other attribute my sinful murmurs only to bodily weakness. Make me bear humbly with the one, and fight honestly against the other. And especially, O my God, pour thy spirit of truth upon me, that my heart may shrink instantly from the least contact with a lie. Make me brave to endure thy holy pain, not thrusting it aside defiantly or denying its power, but simply and quietly as becomes thy child. Grant this, O blessed One, for thy truth's sake, I beseech thee.

38.

Before Death.

O PÈRE tout puissant, n'est tu pas le Dieu qui vis en delà du tombeau comme tu vis en deçà? N'est ce pas ton Esprit de sagesse et d'amour qui recevra mon esprit au moment où, délivré de cette chair infirme et périssable, il entrera dans l'immensité de l'inconnu? Si l'enfant peut se confier sans crainte à son père mortel qui, le prenant par la main, l'introduit dans une demeure où jamais il n'a pénétré, avec quelle confiance filiale, avec quel abandon sans réserve, puis-je, O Père immortel, m'en remettre à toi, certain que tu me conduiras sûrement, et que ta pensée qui dirige les soleils dans les cieux, qui sur la terre guide les nuages et prescrit son chemin à la foudre, saura me diriger, moi aussi, et me guider vers une nouvelle sphère d'activité ! Ta providence, O Dieu, ne saurait être inférieure à la prévoyance d'une mère, qui à l'approche du terme où elle recevra son enfant, lui prépare avec soin son berceau. Ainsi tu prépares leur place dans le monde à venir à ceux qui sont rappelés du monde actuel. La mienne aussi est prête, grâce à tes soins infinis, et je puis adresser avec calme et sérénité mes derniers adieux à cette terre où tu m'as comblé de tant de bienfaits.

PART II.

THE INNER LIFE.

Part II.

THE INNER LIFE.

1.

In the Wilderness.

I KNOW not, O God, how to address thee aright, and yet my soul craves to pour out its doubts and its penitence at thy feet. The creed of my childhood has failed me like a broken reed. Its evidences have proved false; its revelations, mistakes; and the hopes of Paradise with which it lured me to virtue, and fears of Hell wherewith it scared me from vice, have become to me as dreams when one awaketh. In my doubt and my despair, I have wandered far from the path of right. I have failed to keep true even to my own poor thought of duty and honour. I am sinking into a bottomless morass of selfishness and hardness of heart. O that I could arise and retrace my steps, and be once more worthy of my own esteem! I know not if it be possible for me thus to begin to live anew, but at least I will attempt the arduous task. Earnestly and solemnly, here and now, I resolve to be henceforth true and kind and just and generous. I will do what is right, and be what is good, though there be no life beyond the grave, and if thou, O great unknown Lord of all, regardest not from thy high heaven our helpless struggles upon earth.

Creator, Master! Wilt thou not aid me? Is it not thou who hast given me these better thoughts to-day? I can dare to ask thy help in this undertaking, whether thou art the God whom my parents taught me to worship, or the God whom I seem dimly to discern behind this universe and in the depths of my soul. Help me, O thou Almighty One, to keep my resolution. Help me to overcome the temptations which beset me. Help me to be faithful to the law which thy hand, my Creator, must surely have written in my heart.

2.
On the Right Way.

O GOD, I thank thee, I bless thee, with gratitude unspeakable, for the joy of this renovated life. Again I have faith in things holy and noble. Again I know that virtue is a reality and not a dream. There are such things as goodness and unselfishness on earth, and surely, O surely, there is a Righteous Lord on high.

3.
Is Doubt Sin?

O GOD, thou who seest my heart, thou knowest that I long for truth more than they that watch for the morning. If I do not deceive myself utterly, there is nothing on earth which I would not give to know the truth concerning thee. Surely then, O God, I do not sin, even when I question all things, and reject the creed to which millions, wiser and better far than I, have bowed,—the creed on whose acceptance I have been taught that my eternal life depends? O God, my heart bears witness for me. Weak and sinful as I am, I do honestly desire only to believe what is true and to do what is right. Father in heaven, I cannot offend thee whilst I feel thus.

4.

God afar off.

O GREAT, incomprehensible Being, whosoever, whatsoever thou art! Orderer of the world, ultimate source of existence! My soul faints when I think that it is to thee that I dare to speak. I cannot prostrate my spirit into any attitude befitting such a creature as I, addressing such a Being as thou art. I waver and am dumb, doubting if it be possible that my imploring cry could ever pierce the infinite abyss between me and thee. What am I in thy sight? If thou art indeed careful of thy creation, and yearnest like a man over the work of thy hands, even then what am I but the worm under the wheels of thy chariot of immutable law, the mote which trembles in a ray of thy beams?

. . . .

O Lord God of my life, thou whom I worshipped at my mother's knees, and to whom my childish heart went up in trust and confidence: O God, thou art still my God, still nearer to me than all beside. My intellect may learn to measure the abyss between creature and Creator, and my flesh and heart may fail as I consider it. But yet I am thy child. I am what thou hast made me. That is my claim on thee, Lord of the Heavens. Thou art yet the strength of my heart; thou wilt be my portion for ever.

5.

Doubt and Faith.

O THOU, unknown, unimaginable God! dare I speak to thee, dare I lift my thoughts to thee? My feeble aspirations to feel after thee and find thee, are weak and vain as the desire of the moth for the star. Thy nature is beyond the grasp of my intelligence; even thy creation overwhelms me with its awe and with its wonder. When I labour to climb up to the conception of thee by the giant stairs of the ages of geology, or the illimitable galaxies of astronomy, my soul falls down abashed, and I gasp in helplessness and dismay. When I would seek thee through the mazes of metaphysic demonstration, my brain swerves and totters, and refuses to overleap the walls of Time and Space, wherein I and all my race are imprisoned. The farther I press onward, the more hopeless grows my search; and the feeble light, which seemed to guide me at the entrance of the abyss of thy greatness, fades away and leaves me in darkness, solemn as the grave. Is there indeed a God, a Living Will, in this great silent universe? Or are there only Forces and Laws; and powers mindless, loveless, relentless as the winds and waves? There is evil on earth, and sin and pain and wrong unutterable. O God, why are they here? Why, if thou art, and if thou carest for the works of thy hands, dost thou suffer tyranny and cruelty and disease and guilt to ravage thy world?

O Lord of my conscience! thou Holy Spirit whose voice I have heard all my life long in the deepest depth of my soul: thou who orderest me, even me, the creature of a day, to be just and righteous and merciful: thou who hast scourged me with bitter remorse when I have been unjust or unmerciful: thou who hast made it my nature to abhor and despise and loathe wrong and cruelty: thou to whom I cannot pray whilst I harbour one evil purpose in my heart: O thou unseen Master of my will, answer for me the riddle of this painful earth, this dim mysterious universe. The God of Nature I cannot grasp; the righteous Ruler of the world hides himself often behind thick darkness, and bares not his arm even to save the martyr from his fires. But thou, the Lord of Conscience, I find for ever near me. If I shun thee, thou dost follow me. If by my virtue I might climb to heaven, I should find thee there; and if by my sin I make my bed in a hell of remorse, behold, thou art there also. Thy voice speaketh in the roar of the crowd, and thine eye pierceth the thick darkness of my self-deceiving soul. God and Master, I hear that still small voice; I strive to meet that awful and all-seeing eye. I bow before thee as my King: I bless thee as my Lawgiver: I acknowledge thee to be the Lord.

6.

Fiat Lux.

O GOD, with what words of love and gratitude shall I bless thee for the flood of light with which thou hast illumined my heart? No longer is my religion one of duty and reverence alone; but with my whole soul I can love thee, O thou good One! Now, at last, I see clearly the truth I have been blindly seeking so long, even that thy Goodness is that which I feel to be so in my inmost heart, that which spontaneously, joyfully, I love and adore. Hitherto I have called thee "good" and "just," as if the words were but titles of thy Godhead with which my poor thoughts and feelings had nothing in common, and which meant nothing to me. I dared to call thee "just," even while I believed thou didst destine millions of thy helpless creatures to infinite torture for finite transgression. I called thee "good," while I still thought thou couldst look down out of Paradise and see unmoved the agonies of Hell. O Father in heaven, how wild and senseless were such fears! Thou art good, my God, I know it now;

not partially or for time alone, but perfectly, eternally, infinitely! Never has there been through all the past, never will there be in the eternal future, one deed of thine which, could my puny soul know and understand it, would not deepen my reverence and kindle my adoring love. As my dead mother loved me, but more wisely, more tenderly still, even so dost thou, O Father and Mother of the world, love all thy children. Even if I stray from thee, thou wilt never forsake me. Thou wilt punish me and bring me back to thee, and lead me through life and death nearer to thee and more like to thee for ever. O God, I give myself to thee in perfect love and absolute allegiance, for thou art the Lord of my conscience and the God of my heart.

7.

Fiat Pax.
(From the Bengali.)

O GOD, life of the sinful, and help of the helpless: I bow to thee with an humble and grateful heart, for thine infinite mercy to thy sinful child. O Lord, my Father, I thank thee with my whole heart for the endless happiness and peace which fill my soul when I meditate on thy goodness and the beauty of thine ineffable holiness. When the sweet pure light of thy love comforts me even for a moment, then does my dark heart rejoice, and become regardless of all the insignificant pleasures of the world. With a humble and loving heart, I prostrate myself before thee, remembering, O Deliverer of the lost and Way of the wanderer, how thy voice did call me back, and thy light re-illumined hope in my soul, when I had fallen under the temptations of earth and drunk the poison-cup of sin, and when my days had become burdensome through the bitter reproach of conscience, and darkness was spread over all my life. O Lord, the Purifier of the contrite heart, I thank thee that thou makest my soul a habitation of peace, penetrating all its depths with thy tender and mother-like love. Lord, so secret and wonderful is that love of thine, that thou leavest us in ignorance of half its tokens. Merciful One, it is in reverent homage and gratitude to thee for that unasked, unmerited love, that I enjoy the blessings of life. Father, I prostrate myself before thee, and bless thee again and yet again for thy measureless love. Never dost thou display it more tenderly than when thy child, troubled and afflicted, calls on thee alone, kneeling in his lonely chamber, and thou wipest the tears from his eyes, and takest all care and sorrow from his heart, and sayest unto him, " Fear not, my child."

8.
Thanksgiving for Religious Truth.

JE te remercie, O mon Dieu et mon Père, de m'avoir tiré des ténèbres de la tradition, pour m'éclairer de la lumière précieuse de ta vérité. Combien mon cœur était vide et oppressé, combien mon âme était dépourvue de nourriture, quand je t'adorais encore sous la forme d'un homme, quand je te croyais loin de moi, quand je supposais un abîme entre ton cœur paternel et le cœur de ton enfant! Quel bonheur aujourd'hui de te connaitre et de t'aimer comme le Dieu Esprit et infini qui remplis l'univers!

Quelle joie de savoir qu'en parlant de toi il n'est pas necessaire de songer au passé, et de dire que tu t'es révèlé autrefois, que tu as parlé autrefois, que tu t'es incarné autrefois ; mais qu'il est permis de dire que tu te révèles aujourd'hui de la même manière que du temps de nos pères, que tu nous parles aujourd'hui comme tu as parlé aux prophètes de l'ancienne alliance, que tu t'incarnes aujourd'hui en tous ceux qui t'ouvrent, comme Jésus, un cœur pur !

Puissé-je, O Dieu, ne pas me rendre indigne de la grace immense que tu m'as accordée ! Puissé-je ne pas seulement te connaitre par l'esprit, mais te sentir par le cœur ! Que ma vie toute entière porte l'empreinte de ton sceau, et devienne pour mes frères une source de joies et de benedictions.

9.

For Faith.

O GOD, my Father, who art more ready to hear than we are to pray, I entreat thee to bestow on me the precious gift of a lively faith.

Look down upon my soul, and see how blind it is. To me, that which is unreal is ever apt to appear real; while I often scarcely perceive thee, who alone dost truly exist and endure. And if now and then I have a bright glimpse of thine all-encompassing presence, it vanishes quickly, and I return to my state of illusion. Lord, since my spirit is akin to thy Spirit, and since thou hast created me capable of seeing that which is invisible, fix my gaze, I beseech thee, above and beyond this world of sense, which too much intrudes upon me, and teach me in future to walk by faith and not by sight. Lord, I believe; help thou mine unbelief! Open my eyes to see and know thee as my Father, and as the Cause of all that is great and beautiful and real in the universe. Then the world of outward appearance will cease to be so absorbing as it now is, and I shall begin in truth to live. Grant that with clearness of soul I may believe in thee as I believe in my own existence, and that the consciousness of thy never-failing love may abide with me for ever. O my Father, dispel the clouds of sin and selfishness which hide from me the light of thy constant presence. May I realize that pureness of heart without which we cannot see thee. Let me walk with thee every hour of my life, and may faith defend and sustain me until the gates of death shall disclose to me the glorious visions of eternity. Amen.

10.

The Supreme Teacher.

O HOLY and infinite God, how mighty is the thought of thy greatness; is it possible I can realize a part of the wonderfulness of thy glory? Even now as I pause to meditate in the quiet night, it seems to me my thoughts of thee were never so solemn, so full of awe. There have been times when I have turned to earthly teachers, when I have asked of this one and that one, "Lead me to God;" for I have thought I could not reach to thee alone, that others stronger than I must guide my footsteps. And, my Father, they have truly helped me; they were thine elder children, and I needed their help and guidance. I thank thee, Father, for the lessons these thy saints have taught; I thank thee for the light they have brought to the weak and erring; but when their lessons were taught, there was something still needed; they have led me near thee, but I could not find thee with the help of earthly teachers only; and while I relied on them, I had not strength to find thee, thou who art alone in thy majesty and power. I thank thee, too, for that saint, that child of thine, who trod once the shores of Galilee; his faith and his love have taught me; and poor should I be without his teachings. But if I read aright his life's lesson, it teaches me to turn from him to thee. I leave him, I leave all, and alone I cast myself down before thee who art alone. Then, as never before, do I feel thy majesty and power; then do I come nearer to the tenderness of thy mercy. I find thee in all around me, within and without. It is not three times thou art manifested to us, O Lord, nor three hundred times, but in myriads and myriads of times and manners. Wherever we live and move, we see thy wondrous manifestations; and mighty, and alone, and above all, we find thee to be, O Lord, also. O God, thou alone art my Saviour. If others have helped me, it was because thou gavest them power and inspired them. Thou only art my Teacher and my Helper; thou alone my Ruler and my Guide. And what unspeakable joy wells up within me when I find that, weak as I am, I may turn alone to thee! With what blessed swiftness does my soul fly towards thee, now that there is no veil before her which a sainted teacher must lift away! Divided no longer by turning here and there, the whole current of my being flows to thee. O my Father, let it never turn away, but flow onward and onward evermore.

11.

Why God is loved.

O GOD, make me love thee, not only because thou fillest my life with joy, but because thou art infinitely, absolutely, unutterably good in thine own awful nature; because thou lovest all my fellows upon earth, all my brethren in the stars; and because even for me thou wilt seek better things than happiness, and guide and teach and punish me, till I am fit at last to be indeed thy child. Like the Moslem of old, I cry to thee: "Thou art to me all that I desire. Make me to thee what thou desirest, O thou the most Merciful of the merciful!"

12.

The Nearest One.

O GOD, there were years when I was lonely and sorrowful, and had none to love me on earth, and then I thought continually of thee, and talked with thee in the chambers of my heart. And now thou hast made my way bright and joyful, and hast given me near and dear ones, and filled their hearts with tenderness for me. But O, my God, in the midst of my happiness I often forget thee, and my thoughts converse with my human friends, and less and less with thee, thou Almighty Friend.

I deserve that thou shouldst make me feel

lonely once again. Is it not still thou, O God, who alone art truly near me, who alone knowest how little I deserve to be loved, and yet lovest me better than all? In the inmost depths of my spirit thou only canst penetrate; and surrounded by a thousand friends, life would be a solitude but for thee.

Thou art near me now in health and joy. Thou wilt be near me in sickness and grief. And when death comes to sever all other ties, it will but leave me alone with thee. Thine everlasting arms will be round me as I lie down to sleep, and I shall awake from the dream of earthly interests to the reality of thine eternal love.

13.

The Awfulness of God.

O LORD of Heaven, great God of all, I would fain raise my thoughts to the footstool of thy throne. Too often, O mighty One, have I dared to address thee with a mind but half solemnized by the sense of thy majesty, and a heart unabashed before thy holiness. Pardon me, O Lord. I am but a creature of clay, living out here for a few years my narrow, sinful life, full of pollution in my best aspirations, and for ever falling short even of my own poor standard of duty. Clogged and stained with all the past, I know myself utterly unworthy of thy love. I am sinful, and cannot even feel my guilt. I am weak and helpless, and I cannot find strength of will to grasp thy hand outstretched to lift me up. Merciful God, if there were any bounds to thy goodness, any end to thy love, I could have no hope. When I think of thee by the revelation of my understanding alone, I see thee far away beyond all worlds, before all time, giving to the heavens their laws, and filling with thy presence eternity and infinity. And more awful, more tremendous still, O God, art thou when my intellect is silent, and only my conscience bids me bow before thee, the infinitely holy One, before whom the heavens are not pure, and yet who seest all the scars of my past sins festering upon my soul, and all the double thoughts, and longings for forbidden joys, and low, base desires, and selfish affections, and miserable vanities, which make up the sum of my life. Only can my mind and my conscience dare to turn to thee through thine own revelation to my heart that thy goodness is infinite as thy greatness, and that thou, the Lord of the universe, dost love us all, even such as we are now, poor and weak and sin-stained,—lovest us perfectly, infinitely, with more than a father's care, more than a mother's tenderness. O God! Father, Mother, All! melt this cold heart, I implore thee, so that I may not be utterly dead and senseless before such goodness. Give me life, O God, by any teaching thou seest best; only give me life and the power to love thee. Father, come to my heart: I open it to thee. I desire to lie wholly in thy hand, to submit myself entirely to thee, to be purified as thou wilt, and then blessed as thou wilt. Blessed Father, every prayer I can form is summed up in one: Make me love thee better.

14.

For Pardon of a Careless Life.

CREATOR and Master, Almighty, Awful God, I have sinned against thee very grievously. My prayers have been heartless and thoughtless. I have forgotten thee in the work and in the pleasure of my life. I have neglected many of my duties, and have performed others from sordid motives. I have wasted the time and the powers with which thou hast entrusted me, and which I have again and again solemnly dedicated to thy service. I have allowed a thousand evil feelings to harbour in my heart. O God, I lay all these sins, and all the sins of my life, at thy feet. Do to me as seemeth good in thy sight. If I ought to suffer, behold I bow myself to thy righteous and blessed will. Only, O Lord my Father, for thy dear love's sake, aid me, I implore thee, to return wholly and heartily to thee, to forsake my base and hateful sins, and to love thee henceforth with such sustained and fervent love as shall keep me from future transgression.

15.

Sin and Sorrow.

MERCIFUL God, I come to thee bowed to the earth with shame and sorrow. I have failed: I have grievously sinned. . . . .

O God, it is utterly vile of me thus to break the blessed and holy laws which I have learned to know and to revere, and to sin against thee, thou all-good, all-loving Father. I deserve heavy retribution, for I have known my Lord's will and I have done it not. O God, I know that thou forgivest always, and lovest thine erring creatures through all their sin and misery. It is this love of thine which makes my sin and my ingratitude so unutterably base. Help me with thy spirit, Lord of life, to repent bitterly as I have need, and to cast away all the evil which clings around my soul.

16.

From the Depths.

O MOST holy and awful God, who knowest all the secrets of my heart, I have sinned against thee most grievously, I have chosen evil rather than thee, and now I dare not lift up my eyes towards thee. I am bitterly ashamed, and my heart will not open to thy restoring love. For very shame I dare not confess my sin to thee, nor appeal to the love which I have outraged. I have . . . .

. . . .

O thou just and righteous God, make me repent, truly, humbly; make me patient while this darkness lasts, and make me confess that my punishment is just, and that I most richly have deserved it. Father, it is not thou who hast taken away thy glorious light from me, but I who have drawn darkness upon my soul. But, O Lord my Creator, without whom I am not, remember, I pray thee, my littleness and weakness. My heart is not all vile, for thou madest it. Teach me to repent truly. My soul yearns for thee. It is faint and weak, but thou canst restore it. I ask not for forgiveness; only that thou wilt help me out of the snare into which I have wandered, and lead me back to thee by the thorny path of penitence and tears. Do with me what thou wilt, O God my Father; for, weak and sinful, I am still thy child.

17.

Against Thee, Thee only.

O HOLY and awful God, teach me to deplore, not so much this actual sin, though it is grievous, or the consequences of it, though they are bitter; but teach me fearfully to deplore that my heart should choose evil rather than thee. Give me, I pray thee, a heart that shall choose good and resist evil, that shall harbour no wicked thoughts and crave no sinful pleasures. But, O most merciful God, turn not, I implore thee, thy face from me. Teach me my littleness before thee. Make me more tolerant of weakness in others, more tender in judging them. Make me feel how truly all I have is from thee.

18.

Human Love the Key of the Temple.

FATHER, thou knowest how weak I am, and how my heart swerves and falters for ever on the road to thee, and months and years pass on, and I repent a thousand times, and make fresh resolutions of better obedience, and yet at the end am scarcely nearer to thee than at first. To-day it has come to me to learn that I have been all this time living so far from thee because I have not drawn near enough to thy children, but have been following a hard law of duty towards them, instead of thy dear law of love. O God, open my heart to this wider, sweeter charity. Let me put myself and my rights and my duties on another footing than I have hitherto done in my thoughts, and think, not so much what I ought to do for my neighbour, as what I may be allowed to do to bless and help any child of thine. If any one treat me unkindly, instead of the hard effort to pardon the wrong, let me grieve only for the breach of good-will, and try all I may to heal it again; or, if it may be so, to conceal and forget it from the first. O Father, make me recal always how much thou hast forgiven of my ingratitude and disobedience, and how thou lovest me still, unworthy as I am; and then I shall be able to love those who can never sin against me as I have sinned against thee. Help me to lead a life of love and sympathy and generosity; and so make my cold and narrow heart fit at last to be thy dwelling-place. Let me live in love, and live in thee, thou God of Love.

19.

For Spiritual Growth.

O LORD God, my Creator, by thy will I came into being, and at thy command, when the right hour is come, I shall one day leave this world. Thou alone knowest the holiness that I might have attained to, if from my earliest days I had continually obeyed thee, and if I had always claimed the privileges of my sonship. But, O Lord, I have not done so. I have not lived in the strength of thy grace. Thy image is impressed but feebly upon my soul. Yet thine ideal for me still remains. My Father, I beseech thee to form me into it more and more in the years that I have still to live. I place myself in thy loving hands. Work me as on the potter's wheel. Mould me by thine almighty power. Burn out of me all that is sinful and corrupt. As the grass and the flowers grow by means of the warmth of thy sun and the showers of thy rain, so let thy Spirit effect in my spiritual nature a holy growth, that I may become well pleasing in thy sight. Lord, I depend in this upon thy help. Teach me how to will and to work with thee. Every day may I increase in self-forgetfulness, in simplicity, in courage and in trust, and thus shall I every day approach nearer to thy likeness. Without growth there can be no life. Make me, O my God, a true branch of thee, the living Vine, and to thee be all the glory. Amen.

20.
For Strength.

LORD, deliver me from my sins, relieve me from the agony of remorse. Inspire me, God

Almighty, with strength and energy, that I may triumph over temptations, and preserve my soul safe against their encroachments. I am weak; my heart fails me. O Lord, make be strong, that I may never swerve from thee. O thou Father of the fatherless! O thou Helper of the helpless! lay on my troubled heart thy balmy hands. Vouchsafe unto me forbearance and patience, that I may meekly suffer my calamity, and glorify thee even in the midst of tribulation.

Holy God, reveal thy benign face before me, and fill me with courage and enthusiasm. Fix my heart in thee, O Lord, that the face of mortal man may not daunt me. Make truth dearer to me than life itself.

Teach me, O Lord, to pray without ceasing. Teach me to live and die in prayer. Teach me to seek thee prayerfully, find thee prayerfully, and enjoy thee prayerfully.

21.
For a Devoted Life.

O THOU who hearest prayer, give me a prayerful spirit, and draw my heart into a true communion with thee. It is not by my words that my thought is known to thee, for thou seest my inmost heart, thou knowest my most secret desire. O may thy law so rule within me, that these thoughts, these desires, may be as a true prayer, raising me to a nearer union of spirit with thee, and preparing me to receive the blessings which only thou canst send.

Help me, O Heavenly Father, to make my life a true offering of devotion. May gratitude for every joy, patience under every trial, and diligence in my daily work, be the willing service of my heart and hand. And by all my experience may the treasure of my spiritual life be increased. O shew me how I may share with others the good gifts which thou hast entrusted to me not for myself alone. May there shine even in my life some faint reflection of the infinite wisdom and perfect love of thy providence. Keep me in the sacred bond of fellowship with thy children of every nation and in every age. Touch me with a deep pity for the sinful, with tender sympathy for the tried and sorrowful. Save me from the evil of a cold and selfish or a careless spirit.

Finding thee in everything that is true and fair and good, may my earthly home ever become more dear to me. Loving it for what there is in it of heaven, may I be ready when thou callest me to leave it, trusting still to thy guidance, secure in the shelter of thy love.

O help me, Father, to live in the light of a faith and hope like this. Fix my heart on heaven and heavenly things. Teach me the true meaning and purpose of my life. Help me to live in the spirit of my prayer.

22.

Prayer of one who desires a more equal Walk with God.

FATHER, I thank thee that thou hast unveiled thy face to me, and suffered me to behold the beauty of thy holiness. And when I see thee, I know that thou art my strength, my peace, my consolation, my portion for ever. Then I have no desire but to be one with thee in heart and life, to do and bear all thy wise and loving will. But I cannot long dwell at the height whence I see thee always: I sink only too easily to the common level of a worldly life, where meaner desires re-assert their power, and old temptations charm once more, and visible and temporal things hide the things that are unseen and eternal. And when I would fain fly upwards to the clearer air of thy presence, my strength fails me; till at last I almost lose the desire to rise above the dull round of habitual duty, the blinding mists of common interests and passions. Then, O God, I see thy face no more, till from thyself descends a season of refreshing, and the parted clouds again reveal the Sun of my soul.

O Father, at least shew thyself more often to my chilled and darkened spirit, even if it cannot be that I should see thee always. Give me strength and courage to abide always where thou dwellest, in the region of humble self-forgetfulness and true self-sacrifice. Fill me with noble hopes and large purposes for mankind; make my heart to glow with ample charities, and mould it to a fine courtesy. Strengthen me to love what thou lovest; to abhor what thou abhorrest; to do thy will with a joyful courage; and whatever burthens thou layest upon me, to bear them bravely even unto the hill of crucifixion. Only let me be near thee in thy work and will, and peradventure I shall see thee in thy brightness. When the season of less buoyant hope, and feebler energy, and a faith that sees thee no more, but can only feel after thee if haply it may find thee, again darkens upon my soul, help me to recollect thy former goodness with true and lively gratitude, and to remember how, after the leaden clouds and the driving rain, always returned the cheerful sun and the endless depths of heaven. And even if these seasons of clear shining be few, and separated by many dreary days, give me grace to remember the eternal noon of a life to come, in which I shall know even as I am known, and so make myself ready for that beatific vision by faith and fidelity.

23.
Communion with God.

O MY God, I thank thee that thou hast been with me in all my struggles to lay hold of thy truth; that thou hast borne with me in my weaknesses and ignorance; that thou hast strengthened me to endure reproach rather than conform to what is not of thee; and that thou hast opened out to me free and happy communion with thyself. Thou shewest me thy all-sufficiency. Thou hast revealed to me that into thy hands, as a beneficent and ever-watchful Creator, I may commit myself unceasingly. I see how thou rulest over thy works in the perfectness of thy ways. I know that not the least atom thou hast created is overlooked. I am conscious of much evil and infirmity in myself. But that casts me all the more upon thee. None can overcome and deliver me from this evil but thyself. Thou art more conscious of it even than I am. I do not shrink from thee as a vengeful Judge. I come to thee for help and remedy, and know that I come not in vain. Reveal to me all thy will as concerns myself, and give me strength to submit my ways to thee. I forget thee in the midst of the daily concerns of life. Thou never forgettest me. O bring thyself in remembrance to me continually, that I may discern thy hand always in all things. Let not my short remaining time on earth pass away in heedlessness. Cultivate my thoughts, govern my actions, feed my spirit, satisfy my longings which are towards thyself. And so keep before me my happy privilege of being one whom thou hast made and reserved for everlasting blessing.

I thank thee that all creation may thus rejoice in their Creator; and I pray thee to dissipate every error that clouds thee from the view of so many who should know thee as thou art; and that thou wilt reveal thyself to all who seek thee in the completeness of thy perfections.

24.

Thanksgiving, Spiritual and Temporal.

TO thee, O loving Father, I come to bring my offering of thankfulness for thy wonderful gifts which have made my life so rich. It is a joy to speak of thy goodness and to shew forth thy praise. And this power to thank thee, this knowledge of thee as the Source of all good and blessing, is itself one of the greatest of thy mercies, for which I can never sufficiently thank thee.

I bless thee, Lord, for the dear joy of knowing that thou art indeed a Father, blessing and caring for each one of thy children. With deep desire, I pray that I may never cease to feel this sacred tie of love that binds my soul to thee; love that in thee is infinite in its perfection; love that in my frail and weak heart is infinite in its hopes and aspirations, and its capacities for an ever-deepening and widening life. In the bond of such a love thou art with me in my home, in my worship, in my daily work. Thy love is in the love of my dear ones; in the brotherly claims of a wider human fellowship. Thy love is in the pity and compassion that make my heart bleed for the bitter sorrows of the world; that make me, at least in some sad earnest hours, long and seek to lighten the burden of the sufferings that I am pained to see.

In all, O Father, it is thy love which is the living fountain of joy, the inspiration of my prayer, the source of all my hope. And when I ask my heart what offering of gratitude I can bring to thee for all thy mercies, I know that thou desirest but the gift which is itself a joy to bring,—the gift of filial love, and the service which that love inspires.

Deepen, O Lord, the hidden spring of a true devotion to thee. Open my eyes to see the tokens of thy presence everywhere. Make my weak heart strong in the might of thy indwelling Spirit. Ennoble my poor imperfect work with the desire and purpose of doing it for thee. And O, amidst the changing lights or the gathering shadows of this world, may the clear radiance of thy truth and thy love shine on in my soul with increasing brightness, as I draw nearer to its everlasting Source, and walk more closely with thee.

Bless me, O my Father; guide me and keep me; and make me thine, now and evermore.

25.

Living in Love, living in God.

O MY Father, I bring my prayer unto thee. I know that thou wilt help me if I ask thee.

Help me to make my life full of love, perfect love towards thee and those among whom thou hast placed me. I know that I could never love thee aright, did I not also love them faithfully. I would love and serve thee truly, for I love thee, my Father; but I need to feel thy love, else mine might wax faint and feeble. Help me to keep the great truth ever bright before me, that thou lovest me always. Help me to keep my heart constantly filled with thy love. Then I should feel no task hard, no love towards others a difficulty. Then should I be satisfied and cheerful, though sorrow and care should come to me. Then should I be content and at rest in the midst of labour and trial.

Thou only art my Lord and my Shepherd; thou art my Master, my Guide and my Friend; may I be for ever and ever thy servant and thy child, and never wander away from thy side. It is not possible for me to feel any fear before thee, for I know that thou doest always what is best for me. I would trust thee with a perfect trust. As a child puts his hand in his father's, and follows him without a care, so would I follow gladly whithersoever thou shalt lead me. Help me, Father, that I may keep the lamp of my love for thee ever bright with a constant flame; help me, that I may be always ready to see and know thy love that for ever surrounds me.

26.

The Mystery of Sin.

ALMIGHTY God, my soul is heavy and perplexed, for the awful mystery of sin lies heavy upon it. Father, I would not pry into what thou hidest from me, or claim more of thy Light than thou seest fit to grant.

But why, O my Lord, shewest not thou thyself to others as thou hast shewn thyself to me, to bless me so abundantly? If I love thee, O my Father, it is because thou hast poured thy holy love into my soul. Father, *they* would love thee too if they knew but how. I know, my God, that thy mercy is over all thy works; that the love I feel towards my fellows is nothing to the love thou bearest them. Teach me, O Father, to trust all to thee; teach me to proclaim the love thou hast given me; and, troubled as my heart may be, teach me, O holy and most merciful God, to lift it up always in humble thankfulness to thee.

27.
The Father of All.

O FATHER of all the races of men, Father of the whole great human family, how have we darkened and obscured thy face! Everywhere hast thou shed thy heavenly light, and we have blinded our eyes, and then have said that we could not see it. We have dreamed that the sun of thy truth shone only upon our own little strip of land, and that beyond was outer darkness. But how utterly different do we find thee to be, O Lord, when we see that thou who art our Father art also Father of all; that everywhere there is light from thee, if men will but perceive and use it; that all paths shall lead to thee that are trodden in love and purity. Then, O God, do we know thou art great, with a greatness before unknown to us; then do we know indeed thou art loving, leaving none alone in the darkness.

28.
Joy in God.

O ALMIGHTY and merciful God, I tremble before thee, for the sense of thy great goodness overwhelms me. O holy Father, sanctify my joy, I beseech thee, that it be not a snare to me. Thou hast filled my soul, and, as I lie awake, gladness wells up in my heart towards thee. Teach me how to serve thee better; make my heart large to receive thine awful love. O Father, so many of thy children are longing even now for thee, and know thee not; and yet thou loadest me—me, thy sinful, erring child—with thy richest mercies. I know that it is not of my desert, but of thy love, that thou hast blessed me so abundantly. Make me grateful *always;* and when dark days come, and sickness paralyzes my soul, let the thought of thy mercies be with me, and keep me brave and true to glory still in thee.

I am thine, O God. I do trust and worship thee. Make me pure and true, and loyal to thee, my God; and take away all vain thoughts and foolish wilful pride from my heart, I beseech thee.

29.

The World of Love.

FATHER in heaven, I thank thee for the lovingness of thy world towards me; for the lovingness which thy children have shewn me, thy people have revealed to me. Father, I pray thee enlarge my heart and open my soul to receive all these riches which thou hast bestowed on me. Teach me to seek thee in all thy mercies. Pour into me such abundance of thy love, that all my thoughts may be filled with thee. And, above all, let me not selfishly keep to myself thy holy gifts; but teach me how to make others share the glorious riches of love which, in sacred trust, thou hast given me so abundantly. Make my whole life one grateful, loving service, that I may feel I am really thy child, and know that thou art indeed my Father.

30.

Life with God.

O LORD, my God, whose eye searcheth for truth and purity of heart, turn me now away from every vanity of thought, and draw forth some living light of trust and love, that I may meet thee, spirit to spirit, the weak to the Almighty, the sad and sinful to the only Blessed and Holy. O thou Well-spring of eternal life, I bring to thee the thirst I cannot quench: send the cooling drops which shall abate the fever of vain desire, and baptize me unto peace with thee.

O thou Ever-present! there is no faithfulness gentle and long-suffering as thine. All my unrest of soul cometh only hence, that I keep not close to thee, nor lay myself freely open to thy ready help. Thy calmness is ever by to swallow up my fretful cares; thy silent look, to chide my eager words; thine infinite purity, to put to shame whatever is mean and low. Every hour of eternity is full of thee. There is no desert place in life or death where thou art not. It is we alone, O Lord, that stray and change;

and when our faithless spirits would return to thee again, thou stretchest forth thy hand and comfortest us. Never may I forget thee till sin has made thee terrible. Hold not thy peace too long with me, O thou All-merciful, but chasten me betimes, ere I have ceased to lay thy will to heart. O thou Eternal, in whose appointment my life standeth, thou hast committed my work to me, and I would commit my cares to thee. May I feel that I am not my own, and that thou wilt heed my wants while I am intent upon thy will. May I never dwell carelessly, or say in my heart, "I am here, and there is none over me;" nor anxiously, as though my path were hid; but with a mind simply fixed upon my trust, and choosing nothing but the dispositions of thy providence. Before thee, O Lord, I have no rights, save to serve thee with my toil, and love thee in my soul. Yet often have I coveted my rest before the time, and have stretched forth a hand to gather it as the hasty fruit before the summer; and so it has been small and bitter to the taste. Henceforth I would wait upon thy seasons, and leave myself to thee. More and more fill me with that pity for others' troubles which comes from forgetfulness of my own; with the charity of them that know their own unworthiness; with the alacrity of mortals that may not boast of the morrow; and the glad hope of the children of eternity. Lead me in the straight paths of simplicity and sanctity; and may neither the flatteries nor the censures of men betray me into a devious step. And when the last dimness steals upon my eyes, and draws the veil to hide all earthly light, give me to see in the spirit the gracious angels of thy mercy ready to bear me from the scenes of time, and feel a spring of joys permanent as the numbers of eternity. And unto thee, the beginning and the end, Lord of the living, Refuge of the dying, be thanks and praise for ever. Amen.

31.

Love and Serve.

O MY loving Father, I am not content to serve thee and do the work thou hast given me to do. I desire to abide in thee, and enter into the joy of holy communion. Thou art more than a Master; thou art my Father and Friend. While, therefore, I obey thy will as a devoted servant, I would give my love, my heart, my life unto thee, and rejoice exceedingly in thy company. The very thought that thou art near me must give me joy, or thou art not dear to me. Thy name must be sweeter far to me than any other sound, however pleasant, or my heart has loved thee not. As the hart panteth after the water-brooks, so must I seek the light of thy countenance at all times; for it is sweet to behold the face of my truest Friend and my dearest Father. Consent then, O Lord, to dwell in the recesses of my heart, and graciously guide me and gladden me with the light of thy presence. May it not fall to my lot to offer thee the heartless services of outward morality. Teach me to love thee and thy work, and help me to find strength and consolation and reward in the fact, that thou art in me and I am in thee, united for ever in the ties of love.

32.

See and Hear.

AS my outward eyes drink the light of heaven, so grant, dear Lord, that my heart may behold the light of thy presence. And as my ears enjoy outward music, may my soul hear the music of thy word. These two blessings do I humbly beg of thee; thy son needs nothing else to make him pure and happy. The shadow of a distant God, the cold idea of an abstract Deity, satisfy me not; I want the reality, the nearness and the sweetness of thy Presence. Nothing shall stand between thee and my adoring soul. When I pray, may I see thee and commune with thee face to face. When I work, may I embrace and serve thy feet with loving hands. Grant also, I beseech thee, that I may not seek saving wisdom in dead letter, or in the confused teachings of men, but in the living and direct inspiration of thy holy spirit. Speak to me, O my God; I desire to hear thy sweet voice. Let words of truth fall daily upon the ear of my conscience from thy holy lips, and guide me in the right path. When doubts and difficulties arise, mercifully enlighten and inspire me with direct counsel; when I sink into sorrow and despair, revive me with sweet consolation. Speak to me, Lord, in the loving and simple language of a Father, and help me to accept with unfaltering faith whatever thou sayest unto me.

33.

Here and Hereafter.

O MY God, thou art my God here and hereafter. The ties with which thou hast bound me to thee, death shall not break. Our union is everlasting. How I feel comforted and encouraged when I think of this, that thou wilt vouchsafe to deal with thy unworthy servant for ever, and that the blessings of holy communion with thee will be perpetuated for me! It is a joy to serve thee, but infinitely greater is the joy to serve thee with the assurance that the term of my service will never expire. Precious is the privilege of calling thee "Father." How glad then am I that I shall be a child at thy feet for ever! I thank thee, therefore, that thou hast added to my trust in thee a belief in a future life. Lord, I seek no heaven hereafter. I covet no abode of bliss, no outward reward above. To be with thee is my heaven and my salvation, and the only reward I seek. As I abide in thee now, may I continue to live in thee, O Father, and to grow in wisdom and love and purity and joy in thee, time without end.

www.ingramcontent.com/pod-product-compliance
Lightning Source LLC
Chambersburg PA
CBHW022125160426
43197CB00009B/1157